L
too Short
TO
be
ANYTHING
but Happy
AND HEALTHY

LIFE IS
too Short
TO
be
ANYTHING
but Happy
AND HEALTHY

D.L. Mitchell

Library of Congress Control Number:		2019920548
ISBN:	Hardcover	978-1-7960-7739-1
	Softcover	978-1-7960-7738-4
	eBook	978-1-7960-7737-7

Author photo by Jennifer Connelly of Whistling Girl Photography

NASB
Scripture quotations marked NASB are taken from the New American Standard Bible®, Copyright © 1960, 1962, 1963, 1968, 1971, 1972, 1973, 1975, 1977, 1995 by The Lockman Foundation. Used by permission.

NIV
Scripture quotations marked NIV are taken from the Holy Bible, New International Version®. NIV®. Copyright © 1973, 1978, 1984 by International Bible Society. Used by permission of Zondervan. All rights reserved. [Biblica]

Print information available on the last page.

Rev. date: 12/18/2019

To order additional copies of this book, contact:
Xlibris
1-888-795-4274
www.Xlibris.com
Orders@Xlibris.com
712380

To my family and friends, with love and gratitude.
You are my life,
my world,
my inspiration.

CONTENTS

INSPIRED LIVING

Natural Remedies

HEALTHY RECIPES

FOREWORD

GENEROSITY OF SPIRIT is the surest sign of people captivated by the Gospel. You've seen them before. Their lives are a joyful sacrifice. They regularly forget their own needs. They live for others and give without counting the costs. They are the creative minority in our broken world who hold nothing back. To put it simply, we'd be lost without them.

My mom is a part of this creative minority. Her heroic embrace of reality—on God's terms instead of her own—is the secret to her infectious joy. If you're reading this book, it's probably because your life (even indirectly) has been touched by her feminine genius. She is a woman who lives for others and makes generosity look easy.

In the initial pages that follow, Mom will inundate you with practical advice, childlike humor, and wisdom for the ages. It's a summary of her greatest family talks—from the advice she has given me while dating my first girlfriend in high school to the example of faithful suffering she still offers today. In the subsequent sections, her vulnerability and boldness transitions into practical inspirations for healthy living. Though I'm the world's worst chef and rarely see a doctor more than once a year, Mom's natural remedies and healthy recipes are already a source of rich blessing in my life. It's exciting to know they will now be available to the masses.

If you enjoy pondering life's deeper meaning and desire to live with greater freedom and joy, you're in for a treat with this timeless book. Life really is short, and it's better to receive that truth from others than to have to learn it the hard way yourself. Here's to your pursuit of happiness and health in a world full of isolation and noise. Happy reading, my friend.

Jimmy Mitchell
Nashville, Tennessee

ACKNOWLEDGMENTS

D URING THE TIME it has taken to realize the dream of this book, *Life Is Too Short to Be Anything but Happy and Healthy* could not have been published without the help of so many people. I am deeply grateful to all my family and friends who have supported and encouraged me along the way as I embark on writing my first book. So many have given me inspiration, invaluable feedback, and insightful suggestions. From Becky Blythe's first read to every subsequent person who has read my work, I thank you with all my heart for the countless contributions that have made its completion possible.

Three young women in particular have generously and tirelessly edited my first drafts. Special appreciation goes out to Alexander Blythe, who with her steadfast support and vision has given me the inspiration to organize my writings into a prototype of what the book will become. And many thanks go out to Marisa and Gina ValeCruz, who have also given me invaluable edits in the beginning and not only made this a far better book by helping me edit out the bloopers but also added a lot of fun in the process.

I am grateful for my beloved son Jimmy Mitchell for his unending love and support, for his final edits of the "Inspired Living" section, and for writing such a thoughtful and inspiring foreword to the book. I give thanks to Dr. Phillip Sidwell for writing the ingenious foreword to the "Inspired Living" section. To both Donna and Sid, I am grateful for their loving friendship and support over the years; their best friends and my beloved parents, Marshall and Donna Lou Hailey, are smiling down on us. To my beautiful and talented daughter, Haylee Lindenau, I give special thanks for always being there for me, for her brilliant foreword and final edit of the "Natural Remedies" section, and for giving me the greatest joys of this second season of life, my grandsons, David and Liam Lindenau. And to my new friend Hallie Klecker for her bright foreword, invaluable edits, and shining creativity added to the "Healthy

Recipe" section. And finally, to my friend and Pilates Instructor of 20 years, Kimo Kimura, thank you for your insightful book summary and your continued love and support in my life over the past two decades. I couldn't have done it without all of them.

A special note of heartfelt appreciation for the talented Barbara Genner, who has provided the inspiring artwork for the book. Her rendering using the Zentangle method is a simple and beautiful way of expressing one's thoughts and emotions, which is exactly what this book is all about. Also, special thanks to the book editors at Xlibris. Thank you for your dedication and great patience in handling this project with just the right touch. Your consistent motivation and encouragement in completing this book are greatly appreciated.

I thank God daily for assembling these gifted and talented people, without whom the book will have never developed so wonderfully. Thank you a hundred thousand times to all who have prayed for me and my family over the years. I am truly blessed by your love and support.

"Gratitude unlocks the fullness of life. It turns what we have into enough, and more. It turns denial into acceptance, chaos to order, confusion to clarity. It can turn a meal into a feast, a house into a home, and a stranger into a friend. Gratitude makes sense of our past, brings peace for today and creates a vision for tomorrow" (Melody Beattie).

INTRODUCTION

People come into your life for a reason, a season, or a lifetime.

WE'VE HEARD IT said that people come into your life for a reason, a season, or a lifetime. For most of my life, I haven't had any real-life experiences that have given me an empathetic understanding of how profoundly true this statement is. During my life thus far, I have experienced my grandparents' timely deaths at older ages. And I have left behind many dear friends, having moved seven times in my adult life. And sure, there have been plenty of scary trips to the doctor's office and emergency rooms with sick and injured family members. But then within a five-year time span, many of those I have held nearest and dearest to me have gone out of my daily life forever. With the death of both my parents, the end of my vocation as an active mother, the end of a twenty-seven-year marriage, and the death of my eldest son at the young age of twenty-eight, the reality of this profound quote has hit me like never before.

Embracing hope and joy no matter what's going on in life might possibly be one of the hardest things I've ever had to do, as well as the single most important thing I've needed to do to heal and move forward. Accepting life on life's terms has given me the permission and perseverance I need to pick up the pieces and live again. I've grieved, I've reflected, and I've concluded that there is only one real happiness—to love and be loved. I am convinced more than ever that, during every season of life, there will always be "something to do, someone to love, and something to hope for," just as Immanuel Kant has declared as the secrets of a happy life.

I truly feel like I have been blessed my whole life. I have always had something to do, someone to love, and something to hope for. However, it has become more and more apparent to me that this is a choice in life—a daily thing, not a weekend thing, not something we put on hold until later in life, and definitely not something we wait on until the perfect person comes. Love is in our midst and something we need in our life every day. That being said, it is never too late, and there is no time like the present. Although it is certain that people will come in and out of our life, as Christians, we never say goodbye. But we do have to make the choice to love those whom God has blessed us with today and every day, each having the opportunity give purpose and meaning to our life.

So if I truly believe in God's perfect timing and that the key to a hope- and joy-filled life is happy relationships, then what is the blueprint for success? And what am I doing and not doing daily to achieve this? I am certain I will never know the answer to many questions in this life, but there is one thing I am certain of—the one true source to real happiness is being open to giving and receiving the love of those around us every day. If we choose to give thanks in all things and treat others as we like to be treated, we can live a happy and productive life. Likewise, we can and will live in the graces of hope and love.

But life just keeps happening and sometimes seems to get in the way. Imperfect and unpredictable as it is, can we really expect to feel happy every day all day? More than once, I have been able to search my soul and discover a clearer understanding and meaning regarding a personal situation when I have chosen to pray, reflect, and write about it. Sometimes all that is needed is to get something off my chest and onto paper. Other times, writing has helped me prepare for a much-needed discussion. Writing has also given me a great deal of peace and comfort. I attribute my joy, peace, and happiness to the fact that I know God is always there—loving, caring, and listening. And if I'm listening back and the timing is right, His perspective and guidance will show me when I should keep something in my heart, simply let it go, or pursue an action.

I have contemplated writing a book for many years but not really been sure what purpose or message it will bring to others. But then I have realized that if I can make a difference in someone's life for a lifetime or for only a brief time, then it's worth making my mark. God has given each of us very specific gifts as well as crosses to bear, and it is our choice to use them to glorify Him or not. So while I can't imagine that I will ever write a best seller, I have decided that it is the right time and season of life to publish some of my writings, as well as an assortment of my favorite quotes, natural remedies, and healthy recipes.

As I reflect on the first season of life and eagerly await the second, I realize that the people, places, and memories in my life are what hold infinite value. My treasured memories are of the times I've been able to share my life with my favorite people. And the majority of those times are centered on food, drink, and culture. So rather than claim any kind of expertise or self-help advice, I humbly share the following collection of writings, remedies, and recipes, which I have given the title *Life Is Too Short to Be Anything but Happy and Healthy.*

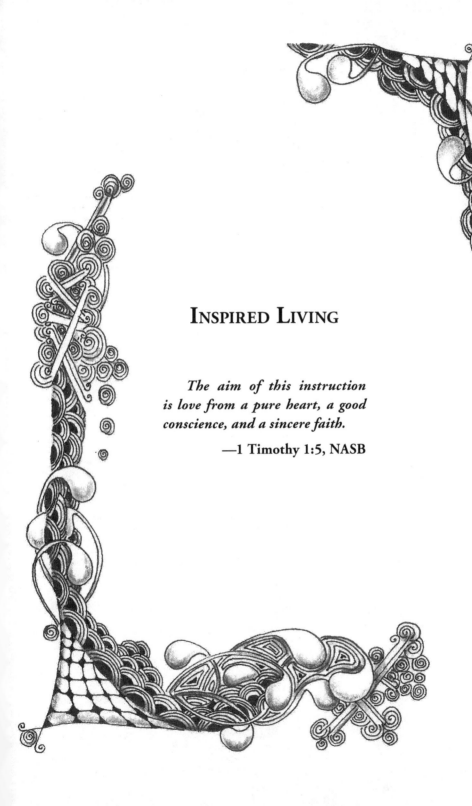

Inspired Living

*The aim of this instruction
is love from a pure heart, a good
conscience, and a sincere faith.*

—1 Timothy 1:5, NASB

FOREWORD

THE THOUGHTS AND insights in "Life Is Too Short To Be Anything But Happy and Healthy" are an excellent understanding of what's involved in living our existence, in our earthly form, in a happy, secure, meaningful life. Her insights, laced with practical recommendations, are corroborated by sound psychological, scientifically evaluated mental processes that prove their effectiveness in creating and sustaining a high quality of life.

Deanna's sharing with the reader is a robust, but deeply thoughtful, discussion of how to apply what we know works to have the life most of us desire. I would urge the reader to take what she is saying and consistently apply her message to your life.

Remember, the only time we have is NOW, moment by moment. The Roman senator Seneca (4 BC – 63 AD) rose in the Roman Forum asking "When Shall We Live If Not Now?" Smart man!

Commonly known as the founder of Positive Psychology, Dr. Martin Seligman launched this revolutionary new field of science in 2004, with his national bestseller, "Authentic Happiness." The most commonly accepted definition for Positive Psychology is "the scientific study of what makes life most worth living."

Life is lived through a series of moments, live life now, it's the only time we have. This is the essence of the widely recommended and used Positive Psychology and Mindfulness approaches in creating and sustain optimal subjective well-being (happiness), meaning, and purpose in our lives.

The various steps along this pathway are well know and scientifically validated.

- The place to start is with counting your blessings
- Identify those things for which you have high levels of gratitude

- Complete a thorough, in-depth physical, mental, emotional, spiritual self-assessment
- Determine your strengths and talents
- Remember the things you have accomplished throughout your life
- Utilize mindfulness processes to optimize your understanding of what is going on inside and around you
- Understand that you create your reality through your perceptions, beliefs, and life experiences
- Clarify your objectives for yourself, your family, for the people who are important to you
- Deepen your faith walk
- Create a vision for your future on how you want your life to be short term (one year from today) as well as for your long term
- What do you want your legacy to be?

You can use this process in conjunction with the application of this excellent book, "Life Is Too Short To Be Anything But Happy and Healthy," for creating and sustaining a high quality of life.

Dr. Phillip Sidwell
Psychologist

CHAPTER I

Seeking Joy

Life does not get better by chance; it gets better by choice.

IN MY SEARCH for joy, peace, and happiness, I have come to realize that although there are many variables, there are some things that are must-haves in my life. Personal success and security comes from feeling good about ourselves and the world around us. This is "an inside job," and no one else can do it for us.

So what does this look like for me? What plan of action must I commit to daily to achieve joy, peace, and happiness no matter what's going on around me? Over time, I have come up with the following blueprint of conditions that simply cannot waver. Trust, honesty, acceptance, openness, forgiveness, and responsibility have to exist in all the relationships in my little world:

- *trusting* God's will and perfect timing over my own and not living in fear of any kind—fear of being myself, fear of being hurt, fear of being vulnerable, or fear of not being enough
- *being* completely open, *honest*, and direct *and* expecting the same from others
- *accepting* and loving myself and others as imperfect as we are, with an open mind and desire for continued growth in all areas of life, especially in giving and receiving God's perfect love
- *opening* my heart and quieting my mind, living in the present, learning from the past, and looking to the future with hope
- *admitting* when I am wrong and asking for *forgiveness*, encouragement, and guidance in improving the error of my ways

- *taking* ownership of my personal *responsibility* and working hard every day at my part in protecting and nourishing my relationship with God and others in my life

Do I adhere to this plan of action every day, and is my little world perfect all the time? Absolutely not. But it is my desire and aspiration to begin and end each day with the goals I have set for everyday life because I know from experience that the joy, peace, and happiness of a conscious and good life will follow suit if I do. And if I put these conditions on hold or allow them to waver for a particular person or situation, the good life I have come to know and love will dissipate.

A. Live Life with Those Who Desire to Be Fully Alive

Most folks are as happy as they make up their minds to be.

—Abraham Lincoln

I T IS MY privilege to share with you a little about my journey and, more importantly, to share encouragement for living a life filled with joy, peace, and hope. And as a result, it will give each of us the feeling of being more fully alive every day.

The first time I truly felt fully alive was with the birth of my firstborn. I thought my heart would burst. It was the deepest emotion of love and joy I had ever felt in my life. Seven corporate moves later, blessed with three children in tow, we finally moved back to our hometown. Living just a few miles from both our parents, with everyone near and dear to us close by, my life was good. If I wasn't with my kids, I was with my parents and if not my parents, my best of friends. Life was a glorious whirlwind filled with love, laughter, and good times. I was living life to the fullest. I never could have imagined how much my life would change in the following decade, not in a million years.

With the death of my parents, the end of active motherhood, and the end of my marriage—*all* within a five-year time span—life just didn't seem all so full anymore. I truly enjoyed all those years of carpool, play dates, field trips, music lessons, concerts, and sports events, and the empty nest was a major adjustment. I had taken care of my husband and children for twenty-five-plus years, as well as both my parents before they died. Suddenly, I felt as if I had no real purpose in life.

But when my eldest son died in his sleep at the young age of twenty-eight, I again felt that my heart would burst, only this time it was heavy with sorrow. Suddenly, my Bobby—who brought life and laughter into every room he entered—was gone from this life, and it felt as if *I was* the one who couldn't breathe. And I certainly had no desire to be among those who wanted to enjoy life and live it to the fullest.

Each day after his death, sitting in the chapel at church, I *was* able to breathe, pray, and gather just enough strength, hope, and courage to face another day, but that was about all I could do. I was so overwhelmed with grief, saddened by the loss of so many loved ones, that for the first time in my life I knew I had no choice but to be still and be with God. I didn't have the energy or desire to make small talk with anyone. I just couldn't put forth the effort. My heart was so heavy, and I felt like I was the one short of breath all the time.

I have chosen to spend much-needed time in prayer and reflection so that I could call to mind all the blessings, not the losses, in my life and listen for direction about where I will be going next on this journey we call life. By the grace of God, I am a living testimony to the adage that "life goes on"; and one day at a time, I am healing and learning again to enjoy this second season of life *among* those who also desire to be fully alive. I *am* persevering in acceptance, peace, and hope by living in the truth and beauty of the gifts that God and life have to offer. Today I live in the peace, hope, and joy of knowing we will share eternal life with our heavenly Father and all our dearly departed loved ones in His perfect timing.

What I've also come to realize is that God is, in fact, preparing us along the way for every step in life. As a wife and mother, He has instilled in me the need for our family to be nourished in mind, body, and soul. To accomplish this, I know instinctively that we need to create community around us so that our environment genuinely feels like home. To do this, I need to get the family involved in our neighborhood, church, schools, and extracurricular activities as quickly as possible. And so I have.

So many different experiences, so many different memories—I won't trade them for anything. My vocation as a wife and mother—along with a love and appreciation for God, family, church, community, and the arts—has prepared me with the basic structure for a mission or rather passion for my second season of life. Today I know that the gift of life and the love of God and one another are truly what give us the meaning and purpose we need to live a full life. As a result of discerning what to do with this heightened awareness, I have become more and more grateful for those people in my life who have been, in fact, living full lives and making the most out of every day. By the grace of God, I have been inspired to gather the strength and courage to share my life experiences in this book. Likewise, in my desire to share all that is good in life, I have created the Fully Alive Outreach, which continuously provides a current network of resources and services in health and wellness, fine arts, and travel.

We all have the opportunity to make many choices every day, but I think the most important one is to wake up with the courage and perseverance to make the most of every day, with a grateful and open heart for the many blessings that come our way, and with the sincerity and authenticity of truly desiring to share our life with others. We just might have to wait for our utopia in heaven, but there is a good life to be lived right here and right now, not in the past and not in the future.

B. When I Got Busy, I Got Better. Wait . . . What?

The best is yet to come.

YES, AT ONE time, I did think that was the ticket—stay busy. I filled up my calendar with my own agenda for good works. And I actually thought that the more I did, especially if I deemed it important, the more worthy I was myself. Somehow I had confused busyness with productivity and self-worth. And as an added bonus, if I stayed busy enough, then I didn't have time to feel my own feelings. I'd be too tired at the end of the day to have the energy or concentration to consider self-reflection or self-examination. Heaven forbid if I took the time to note my responsibility and liability in relationships and life choices. Rather than realizing the grace and mercy of God, I thought my own raw determination would see me through, all the while unwilling to wait on His perfect timing.

Reflecting on the busyness of a full schedule we all sometimes create for ourselves, I truly believe it can be a major cause of the self-centeredness and, likewise, the destruction of relationships in the world today. Just think about how many broken relationships exist because we just don't make time for one another; our own personal agenda takes priority. All relationships need to be nurtured and protected. And if I'm too busy with my own stuff, then eventually the people I don't have time for will fall away from me and fill their life with other people, places, and things.

Stay busy? No way, not for me. I choose to spend my time loving myself as well as all the relationships and opportunities given to me daily, nurturing and protecting each as the perfect gift from God that it is. The more love I share, the more I receive. And that goes not only for people but also for animals and the rest of the world around us.

However, it is extremely important to note, at this time, that there are some people out there who don't want our love and attention, and that's okay. We need to discern regularly who is interested and worthy of our love and affection and who is not. I have once heard it said that if we continue to go to a hardware store rather than the grocery store for bread, we will eventually drive ourselves crazy. Upon reflection, there is great truth to this simple statement. We are all on a unique and individual journey and do not need to be challenged by anyone else's dreams or lifestyles. Likewise, the key to keeping peace and happiness on our journey is accepting ourselves as well as others right where they are. Our lives are richer and fuller when the people we choose to surround ourselves with have similar needs and desires as well as morals and values. This awareness has been proved to me over and over again.

If I stay so busy that I don't hold myself accountable to others or, worse, to myself, I have only served myself, not God and certainly not others. Even at the end of the most exhausting day, we must do a self-examination if we hope to grow or become better versions of ourselves. It is up to every one of us to make a difference in our family, community, and the world. So for me, if I'm going to get busy at anything, it will be to get out of myself and into loving and serving God and others. My salvation depends on it.

You might ask, "Where is she going with this one?" Glad you've asked. The dictionary states that *salvation* is "the saving of the soul from sin and its consequences." It may also be called *deliverance* or *redemption* from sin and its effects. I can only speak for myself, but this might well be a much better choice for my efforts during those times when I think I need to keep myself busy.

In my research of Catholicism over the years, I have discovered in the *United States Catholic Catechism for Adults* how the founding fathers of the Catholic Church explain the meaning of *salvation*:

> The Second Vatican Council [of the Catholic Church] declared that "the future of humanity is in the hands of those men who are capable of providing the generations to come with reasons for life and optimism." (GS, no 31). No one can live without the hope that life has ultimate and lasting meaning beyond the concerns and struggles, the joys and satisfactions of each day. Catholics find that meaning and hope in Jesus Christ, whom God the Father has sent into the world for the salvation of all peoples.

Salvation could certainly never be achieved if we are only concerned with our self-serving agendas. Our daily contemplation followed up with the active involvement of reaching out and giving life to those around us allows for the very existence of future life itself. The peace and security that results from our actions creates the joys and satisfactions of each and every day.

C. Love Is Not on a Schedule

Our lives are a reflection of what we focus on each day.

WHILE SOME PEOPLE enjoy time spent with family and friends building relationships, others prefer time spent alone enjoying solitude—the first kind being relationship oriented, the second being goal oriented. Trust me, I love a good project and am always setting new goals for myself, but I also know for certain that I am relationship oriented. While I prefer to keep family and friends close by being intentional in including them in my daily schedule, I appreciate and understand that there are those who prefer solitude and will not make themselves as available.

Does being in a loving relationship sound like hard work? And if so, why it is that we will work twelve-hour workdays, work out in a gym two hours a day, or keep a house cleaner than Mr. Clean but frown at investing time and energy in our relationships? If we know in our heart that hard work truly does pay off, then we must also admit that if we put all our energies into ourselves, work, or play, our relationships will suffer.

I think we can all sometimes be a little hesitant to make relationships a priority. Because of our own fear, we are cautious to commit and include in our busy schedules the people we've been blessed to have in our lives—fear of allowing someone else in, fear of letting them know us on an intimate and deeper level, fear of being emotionally and physically available to another human being daily. Sure, superficial relationships are easier. But once again, I am reminded that I get out of something what I put in it.

Let's revisit the reality of life choices. If I am relationship oriented and want all of the above in my relationships, then I best be choosing people for my inner circle of life who have the same desires and expectations. Bottom line, I *do* want the relationships in my life to be like a river—always flowing—and not like the ocean, coming and going.

For me, true, authentic relationships are ones in which both parties are held accountable, schedules are made together, and compromises exist because the relationship is considered worthy and important enough to nurture and protect. Anything else creates distance and detachment. Love is not on a schedule, and relationships cannot simply be turned on and off like a light switch, engaging in conversation or activity only when it's convenient. A genuine relationship is something we are both committed to, and likewise, we are continuous and consistent with our efforts. It's dependable, mutually satisfying, and fulfilling. This is the foundation for trust and confidence in a relationship.

Knowing and accepting that there are differences in what we expect a relationship to look and feel like makes it so much easier for me to let go of the unrealistic expectations of those who don't want the same out of life as I do. However, just as I cannot impose my lifestyle on others, they cannot impose theirs on me. Life is a direct result of the individual choices we make, our heavenly Father's perfect gift of free will. We have to be true to ourselves and at the same time allow life to peacefully fall into place. We will be happier and more peaceful if we let go of the outcomes in life and consistently seek God's will in everything and everyone. I look forward to the time when we all live in the complete peace and joy that comes from loving and being loved by God and one another every day, all day. Oh yeah, that sounds like heaven to me.

Not too long ago, I decided to write a prayer that expressed my sentiments on relationships, and I would pray this every day:

> Thank you so much for all Your many blessings, thank You for this day, and thank You especially for the gift of Your son, our Lord and Savior, who taught us pure and perfect love, obedience, and compassion. Please guide and direct us today and always that we may be open and willing to an understanding of Your will for our lives, our relationships, and our future. Please guide our thoughts, words, and actions so that all that we say and do is an open, honest, and true reflection of your love, forgiveness, and compassion. Thank You for the joy, peace, and happiness that comes from loving and trusting You and each other. Have mercy on us, oh Lord. We trust in You always.

D. In God We Trust

> *Be anxious for nothing, but in everything by prayer and*
> *supplication with thanksgiving let your requests be made*
> *known to God. And the peace of God, which surpasses all*
> *comprehension, will guard your hearts and your minds in*
> *Christ Jesus.*
>
> —Philippians 4:6–9, NASB

OVER A COUPLE of hundred years ago, a handful of very wise men have declared that we should incorporate four words as the foundation for the American way of life: "In God we trust." Thank God for their wisdom, foresight, and perseverance. Yet do you ever wonder why so many people are unhappy, even though they could be living the American dream in the best country in the world? Are we too busy blaming everyone else for all our shortcomings and perceived failures? Are we too busy packing as much as we possibly can into every day, just hoping and waiting for life to calm down long enough to start living the life we truly want and hope for? Is this perhaps because we are afraid of self-discovery or trusting others?

For some of us, the thought of trusting a greater power outside ourselves is a threatening concept. This is especially hard for those who have become used to the illusion of being the one in complete control. Worse yet is the group who goes through life thinking it's their destiny to be second best, expecting the worst from every situation, and giving up their birthrights to the control of another undeserving human being. Unfortunately, this group becomes authors of their own misfortune, buying into the false preconception that no matter what they do, it will never be good enough and that they are different and unlovable. Could these misconceptions of who's in control be the cause of unhappiness?

What if we trust God's will for our life rather than continue to superimpose our will over His? What if we make the choice to begin living that life today? Will it make a difference in our outlook or, more importantly, in our actions? Will we feel more at peace with ourselves, with others, with the world? We have quickly jumped on board when

Nike has coined the phrase "just do it" to encourage sportsmanship and health, but are we as enthusiastic about the campaign our forefathers have secured for us in America to live a life whereby *in God we trust*?

Are we willing to believe that the Spirit is leading us every step of the way and that He knows the next best step long before we do, if only we would listen? With trust in God, we can be confident in knowing that we are never alone, and there is no obstacle that hard work and His amazing grace cannot overcome. However, if we continue to think too much or too little of ourselves, we will struggle to be content in spite of ourselves. When we realize that the same God who has created the entire universe probably knows how to repair our broken relationships, help prepare us for our next challenge, and help us resist worldly temptations, then we will be able to tap into the boundless positive energy and hope for living a completely inspired life that is available to us every day.

Whew! What a relief! And to think we have been carrying the weight of ourselves, our family and friends, and the whole world on our own shoulders when all along the Holy Spirit has been in front of us, beside us, and behind us, always willing to help and pick up the slack. When we trust in God, we no longer need to feel the burden of taking on everything or everybody. We are each unique but never alone, and much of what we need to live a happy and productive life is ours for the asking. Many ask, "Then where is God when I need Him, and why does He let bad things happen?" All I can say to those questions is that sometimes—no, all the time, we need to have trust and have faith that everything happens for a reason.

So asking questions is a good thing, but doubting God—well, that is another thing altogether. I am reminded of what a gentleman God is by giving us free will. We have the choice to believe and live in the light or not believe and live in darkness. It is always our choice. However, we also have to acknowledge and accept that we will live with the consequences of our choices, the good and bad ones. I have experienced over and over again that when I let God's light in and live in faith in all things (whether I personally deem them good or bad), His light will consume *all* the darkness within me, allowing me to live in joy, peace, and happiness.

CHAPTER II

Communicating Effectively

The single biggest problem in communication is the
illusion that it has taken place.

—George Bernard Shaw

I F OPEN, HONEST, and loving communication is the key to every relationship—and I truly believe it is—then why don't we choose to make it a priority, and why is it so hard sometimes? No matter how competent we are, most of us avoid conversations that cause anxiety and frustration. We often do not talk about what's bothering us, and then when we finally do talk, things have only gotten worse. Feelings of anger, hurt, and guilt have escalated, and both parties become more and more convinced that they are right and misunderstood. So what makes communication so hard? It goes back to that outrageous feeling of fear. In the case of not communicating effectively, it is the fear of the consequences of the discussion at hand.

I think we all hear and see so much more poor than good communication daily in all facets of life that our fear is justified. And after all, if learned behavior is a dominant influence in the way we ourselves communicate, especially under stress, then how are we going to ever change this ineffective behavior? Unfortunately, we resort to poor communication with those whom we are closest to and most familiar with. Yeah, you've guessed it, usually our family, especially when we are feeling tired, lonely, afraid, or hurt. We save the good communication skills in the back pocket for special occasions. But many times, we just simply forget or neglect to pull them out.

When we feel comfortable and not judged as we express our needs, fears, and desires, the bonds of love and trust are strengthened. This results in a good foundation for resolving conflicts and building healthy relationships. But as soon as we feel awkward or uncomfortable, we talk too much or too little, in both instances pushing others away or shutting down.

I think it is also crucially important to note here that nonverbal cues—such as body language, eye contact, touching, leaning forward or away, and crossing arms over the chest—are equally important in communication, if not more. As the saying goes, "Actions speak louder than words." So if we are looking at a phone, computer, or TV screen when we speak rather than at each other, we are missing a lot of what's being said or not said.

A. "Don't Take Anything Personally." Really?

How good and pleasant it is when God's people live together in unity.

—Psalm 133:1, NIV

TODAY WAS A beautiful day in Atlanta, Georgia, and God's blessings were abundant. The sun was shining, the birds were singing, and the temperature was perfect. But even with all that, the day just didn't start off exactly as I would have liked. With my very first phone call of the day, someone said something that I thought was rude and unnecessary, and I took it personally. What was up with that?

More than a decade ago, I read with my book club *The Four Agreements (A Toltec Wisdom Book)* by Don Miguel Ruiz, in which he described a way of life distinguished by the ready accessibility of happiness and love. The four agreements were (1) be impeccable with your word, (2) don't take anything personally, (3) don't make assumptions, and (4) always do your best. Let's just say that I did not follow the second agreement this morning, and I did take something personally. Hey, I was willing to admit my weaknesses. And thank God, during an open and honest conversation with a dear friend later that day, I was reminded that I did not have to give my serenity and good nature away by succumbing to feeling fretful over someone or something that I never had control over in the first place. By picking up the phone and calling a dear friend whom I loved and trusted, I received the blessing of peace and was able to maintain it during a subsequent discussion with the person who had offended me.

These simple yet profound teachings are based on the four agreements we make with ourselves every day. Sounds easy enough. For me, I think the greatest message I have got from these wise teachings is to let go of other people's stuff. By that I mean taking into action that second agreement. Don't take things personally and, likewise, adhere to the wise mentality of "that's their stuff, not mine, and I don't have to deal with it." If I take it personally, I'm basically agreeing with whatever has been said or done. And as soon as I agree, I'm taking responsibility for everything. Their opinions, beliefs, and points of view are exactly that—theirs, not mine. When I allow myself to take it personally, it becomes mine.

We have the right to walk away from inappropriate behavior and never look back. We don't have to accept it, fix it, and most importantly take responsibility for it. Likewise, we also have to accept that we each have a right to our own opinion according to our belief system, but that does not give us the right to impose our belief system on one another. Seriously, I have received an overwhelming amount of personal freedom from this agreement.

In the scenario mentioned above, I have not initially followed the second agreement. However, on any given occasion, whenever I'm struggling with taking someone or something personally, these original feelings of discomfort can be exchanged for blessings of peace and hope that result from an open and honest conversation with a dear friend whom I trust. Having a support system that I can turn to in time of need and someone whom I can completely and thoroughly trust is essential to my personal success in processing life and relationships daily.

Then when and if I am ready to face my anger, fears, or doubts about something someone has said or done, I am in control of my feelings, and I can calmly and productively state them. In the same way, I am taking responsibility for my belief system and no one else's. I don't have to defend my beliefs or create conflicts. As a result, I am avoiding needless pain and suffering for myself as well as others. Every agreement I have made with myself is a direct result of my thoughts and beliefs, not those of others. I am truly thankful for the gift of family and dear friends whom I have the privilege of loving and trusting with my innermost feelings, beliefs, and desires.

As for my personal well-being, I continue to be amazed at how marvelous it does feel to work through a misunderstanding and how much richer the connection feels in the relationship as a result of the challenge. Yes, it takes commitment; and yes, it takes patience and even endurance, but the result is also so satisfying. My breath is simply taken away when the feelings of peace and hope that come with mutual trust replace the feelings of anxiety and discomfort that come with fear. With trust in God's will and in one another, there is no misunderstanding too small and no challenge too difficult to overcome and conquer.

If we choose to give thanks in all things and treat others as we would like to be treated, we will live in the graces of love and hope.

B. Treat Others as You Would Like to Be Treated

Treat others as you would like to be treated, with the gifts of the Holy Spirit—with honor, loyalty, kindness, honesty, generosity, commitment, and accountability.

YOU KNOW WHAT I'm talking about—the golden rule. We've learned it in kindergarten. Well, actually, I hope we've all learned it even before that. Treat others as you would like to be treated—we know this to be the truth, but why is it just so darn hard sometimes? When I feel like I have given all I have to give and I still feel like I'm getting the short end of the stick, that's when it's hardest for me. I cannot tell a lie. When I feel unappreciated and taken advantage of, it's just plain hard for me to keep on giving.

I remember one of the last times my dear, sweet mother was in the hospital for an extended stay; she had the nurse from hell. Clearly, the nurse was an unhappy camper, but it upset me to see her treat my mother so unkindly. When I finally stated that I was going to say something, dear Mimi said, "No, I don't want you to. I've decided I'm going to kill her with kindness instead."

When I arrived the next day, they were both smiling and enjoying a simple conversation. I asked my mom how in the world she managed to break through, and she told me she noticed a dog pin clipped to the nurse's name badge and asked if she had one. She said, "Oh yes, I have a couple." And once my mom showed sincere interest for the nurse's love of dogs, the nurse was honest with Mimi and said she actually liked dogs a lot better than people. My mom didn't necessarily share the nurse's love of dogs over people, but she accepted and supported her point of view. Filled with forgiveness and compassion, Mimi's friendly and kind spirit brought out the best in that nurse.

Like my mom and her mother before her, it has always given me so much joy to bring family and friends together to share in food and drink. However, that being said, it also creates some disappointment and even resentment within me when it is not received with kindness and gratitude. Likewise, I will slowly but surely withdraw from that person or group of people if the behavior doesn't change, and I continue to feel taken advantage of. My mode of operation is to avoid my hurt feelings and subsequent conflict by removing myself from the situation rather than dealing with it. As I've matured, I realize this behavior isn't allowing me the opportunity to grow from it. So with this personal awareness, this is how the subsequent conversation unfolded when these same feelings have arisen in me after a dinner gathering at the house this week:

"Let's talk about last night. I believe it is fair to say that while we both know what it looks like to be present and interested in the ones we are with, it was completely obvious that you were not truly present and had a different agenda on your mind. The behavior displayed last night might be expected from someone who didn't really care about who they were with but certainly not from family and friends, especially being well aware of what the time, energy, and cost in preparing such an enjoyable evening together would have been."

The apology that followed was preceded with "I'm sorry you felt that way" and ended with "I didn't know you were so sensitive." My reply would always be "An apology is certainly not a justification for wrongful behavior and usually begins and ends with *I*, not *you*." A few exchanges later, a better understanding and acceptance of feelings invoked was eventually achieved.

However, I honestly believe the situation would have come up over and over again had it not been addressed. History will repeat itself if a vested interest isn't made to rectify the behavior. When accountability is taken for words or actions that cause another discomfort or pain, a sincere apology is so easily received and accepted, with the added bonus of a deeper understanding of each other. Without accountability, it just feels like empty words. I think it is equally important to state here that the loving acceptance of a sincere apology, irrespective of reference to being right or judged in any way, is the key to the success of this exchange. Equally important to note is that a successful outcome has to be desired and achieved by both parties involved.

We all need a little reminder once in a while to purify our hearts and restore the desire in each of us to seek His will with all our mind, heart, and soul. God willing, we will all meet that special someone here on the earth (parent, friend, spouse, or child) who will exemplify and share with us the joy of living a life of love, obedience, and commitment—and if not now, then surely in heaven. But life is too short to live with misery, regrets, or even anger. We need to treat each other as we would like to be treated, learn to love, forgive and reconcile, move forward, and then love some more. But let's be honest, sometimes we just have to set some boundaries and clarify what's acceptable behavior and what's not.

C. Sometimes Only Two Words Are Necessary

Manners are a sensitive awareness of the feelings of others. If you have that awareness, you have good manners, no matter what fork you use.

—Emily Post

AFTER NOT RECEIVING a response to a scheduling issue for more than a day or two, and I need to add this was not the first time it had happened with this person, I had no other words for a subsequent discussion than these two words, "bite me." Rude and inconsiderate people tend to bring out the worst in me. But can I also just say here how much better it feels when I express myself rather than hold on to these feelings of resentment? I won't use a strong response too hastily or too often because it will dilute the effectiveness, but sometimes we just have to call a spade a spade. I'll immediately follow this declaration with "I'm sorry, a timely response would have been appreciated. My schedule is just as important to me as yours is to you."

Of course, it's never a good idea to succumb ourselves or coerce others into doing something we don't want to do, but let's be courteous and give everyone in the equation the opportunity of making alternate plans. If we discover that someone frequently won't commit to plans or, worse, changes plans at the last minute, then eventually we'll probably find someone else to make plans with, especially if it's something we really want to do. We're not talking extremes or excessiveness. We're talking about appropriate follow-through within a reasonable amount of time. I have been taught that it's good etiquette to answer communication within twenty-four hours. And I think this applies to family and friends as well. Obviously, with those closest to us, immediate feedback—even if it's two words—is the loving, kind, and considerate thing to do, especially if it involves scheduling. Timely and honest responses free everyone involved to continue with plans, whatever they might be.

Now some folks may be used to what they consider a more independent lifestyle, without accountability or responsibility to anyone or anything. But in a mutually respectful relationship, checking in with each other regularly is the right thing to do not because we feel obligated but because this is the behavior that gives everyone peace, confidence, and trust in each other. And if I reach out to say "I love you" or "I am thinking about you," a reply won't necessarily have to follow; but if it doesn't, one might certainly have good reason to wonder why.

Effective communicators are those who have become aware that trust is their most important asset, and if lost, it takes a lot of time and effort to recuperate. Trust can be lost through any number of things that we might initially consider as small details, such as not responding, arriving late, or not genuinely thanking people. Like most things in life, "an ounce of prevention is worth a pound of cure" as Benjamin Franklin so famously advised fire-threatened Philadelphians in 1736. When we pay attention to the details, clarify our intentions, involve others, and customize our efforts because we have taken the time and effort to become aware of what makes others respond to us more positively, we become more effective and efficient communicators.

Every time we open our mouth, we reveal just a little something more about ourselves to someone else. And it's not just in what we say but also in how we say it. It comes as no surprise that speaking clearly, sincerely, openly, and honestly is always the best policy. That being said, we need to be able to make ourselves heard without interrupting, talking over others, or shouting. We also need to feel free to say what we think and how we feel without the worry of hurting someone's feelings. Good communication is important enough to cultivate, even if we're starting from ground zero. With a little bit of care and effort exercised, we can open up channels for communication or shut them down.

And it's not just about the spoken word; the written word is of equal importance. If we're rushed for time and only a text will do, we need to write it with caution. There is so much room for misunderstanding simply because of the choice of words. In this case, haste makes waste. The amount of time and effort explaining a misinterpreted text can be not only frustrating but also damaging to a relationship. When it's important, a quick phone call might be preferable. Our voice inflection and mannerisms affirm what we're saying or not saying in a way that a text never could.

Let's take this written word to the next level. A good old-fashioned card or letter is still one of the most endearing efforts a person can make to show another how much they care. It is such an awesome but many times forgotten way of expressing our thoughts of love and concern for one another. "Thank you," "Take care," "Get well," "Feel better," "Thinking of you," "For someone special," "You're appreciated," and "You're welcome" are some of the best two or three words we can use when expressing ourselves.

D. Difficult Conversation? Bring It On!

*The effectiveness of communication is not defined by
the communication but by the response.*

—Milton Erickson

D O YOU THINK anybody has ever started off the day thinking, *Today I'm going to take the challenge. I'm going to resolve all the difficult conversations in my life?* Probably not. It's more like, *Today I choose to avoid and put off any and all difficult conversations.* Many times, we agree and even commit to a conversation that needs to take place, but then we put it on the back burner, sort of hoping the issue will just resolve itself or go away altogether. I have come to realize that key areas of sensitivity and pain will continue to resurface if not addressed, and the negative energy stored up behind them seems to intensify. Perhaps we are all just a tad sensitive in that region of our heart where we expect conflict and rejection, and if a conversation is going to cause those feelings to surface, then it's better to put them off as long as possible. Unfortunately, this is not the truth of the matter.

So the question we must ask ourselves is not whether the strong feelings are going to arise, because they will, but how to handle them when they do. Eliminating fear and anxiety altogether might be an unrealistic goal. However, getting better results from difficult conversations is certainly obtainable. Like anything else we tackle in life, practice makes perfect. Just like we can't exercise once and expect to be healthy and fit, the lasting results of good communication come from dedication, hard work, and consistency over time.

When we finally do get around to having that dreaded conversation, one of the most important things we can remember to do is stay on topic. When we lose our concentration, we forget what we have been saying and lose confidence in ourselves as well as the outcome of the conversation. Likewise, if we get sidetracked with the blame and punishment game, our energy goes into defensive behavior rather than understanding the situation as well as another's point of view. And finally, arguing just for the sake of arguing results in a battle of ardent messages that pull us apart rather than draw us together. Ultimately, we have to decide which is more important, feeling happy or feeling right.

Inevitably, what we individually choose to notice and ignore will have everything to do with who we are, what we care about, and what we consider right or wrong. This programming will not necessarily be the same as the person we are talking to. Likewise, the more interested we are in each other's hopes, dreams, and fears, the greater the likelihood of success in all our communication. However, if everything we know is the direct result of the information and experiences we have absorbed in our lifetime and we never investigate whether that information is accurate, we will have acquired ideas that might be imperfect and unreliable. And these ideas might just undermine our ability to enjoy a healthy and satisfying relationship—one in which we feel happy, safe, and confident. So when something is not working, we can usually assume that we are operating on false information. The greatest blessing and opportunity for our personal growth is awareness, coupled with the willingness to make life-transforming changes when necessary.

By taking personal responsibility and contemplation of what works not just for ourselves but also for others, we become accountable to and for the relationships in our life. Then we step up and do something about it. When we take an active role in nurturing and protecting our relationships, we find that we're less afraid of what others might say and have a heightened sense of freedom for action as well as a stronger sense of confidence and self-worth in every conversation.

Today I appreciate and understand that some people, due to their own fear and pain, can't or won't commit to anything but superficial conversations, and that's great for them, but that just doesn't work for me. Similarly, I have discovered that this kind of relationship is very difficult for me to maintain because the people who keep others at arm's length generally aren't open to a deeper and more intimate conversation. And if a conflict arises, the doors of communication close even more. Assuming the thought process here is that all is well in the world as long as there are no expectations, no commitments, and no accountability, this also means that there's no vulnerability, no intimacy, and no genuine love or concern for one another. Unfortunately, this is not very effective for the future of any relationship. The success of any relationship depends on our ability to be open, honest, and truthful in our communications. And when we wholeheartedly believe and trust in God's will, we can live in peace and never need to fear difficult conversations.

In each conversation, we must hold not only ourselves accountable but also each other. It's the only way to grow and mature a little each day while becoming the best person and friend we can be. My grandmother, who was forever repeating clever and witty expressions, used to say, "To have a friend, you have to be a friend." Otherwise known as Little Mommy after the births of my three children, my grandmother was truly everyone's best friend. Always giving and sharing, she would drop everything she was doing just to sit and talk with you. What I remember most about her is her kindness and ability to put everyone at ease, even during the most difficult conversations. I am so blessed to have had her in my life and am grateful for the spiritual wisdom she has passed on so freely.

Difficult conversations might start out feeling uncomfortable, but the result can be effective and fruitful when all parties are interested and committed to a fair and loving resolution. With open and honest communication, even the most challenging discussions can be resolved in genuinely taking care of ourselves and one another. So how do we start that difficult conversation? Here are a few examples of openers that can make it a little easier:

"I haven't heard anything from you. Just checking in, are we still on for . . .?"

"Let me just clarify. What I heard you say is . . ."

"I'm a little out of sorts. I'd like to hear what you think about . . ."

"I need your help with something."

"This sounds really important to you. Tell me more about it."

"From what you've said, I can see how you came to this conclusion. Let's talk . . ."

"I'd like to talk about . . ., but first, I'd like to get your point of view."

CHAPTER III

Processing Feelings

When dealing with people, remember you are not dealing with creatures of logic, but with creatures of emotion.

—Dale Carnegie

WHATEVER THE SEASON of life and all that comes with it, our feelings need to be processed. We have heard and seen enough in the world today of those who seem to be functioning normally and then suddenly explode in anger and do harm to themselves and those around them. Their suppressed feelings, sooner or later, leak out. So how do we deal with our feelings? We need to examine our conscience, acknowledge that our feelings are real, not be afraid of them, and then within a timely manner share our feelings with trusted family or friends. With that in mind, we have to remember that venting is not the same as processing. As needed, we can seek therapists or professionals to work through unhealthy, stagnant feelings.

Let's take just a moment to discuss the difference between feelings and emotions. Our feelings come from the world around us, and they react with our senses, such as happy, mad, glad, sad, hungry, tired, excited, nervous, scared, and disgusted. Our feelings are meant to be experienced for short periods. However, our emotions are feelings that have become a long-term state of mind. If we don't deal with our feelings, they eventually become the emotions that dictate our thoughts, words, and behavior. Likewise, because emotions are internal, we have to change our mind-set to change our emotions, and this process takes time.

The most interesting thing I have discovered when researching emotions is that there are only two basic emotions in life, love and fear. The love-based emotions are emotions such as joy, happiness, compassion, trust, and contentment. The fear-based emotions are anxiety, anger, sadness, depression, loneliness, guilt, and shame.

Not surprisingly, these emotions affect our physical health and wellness. If we ignore, dismiss, or repress our emotions, we are setting ourselves up for a sundry of physical illnesses. Emotions that are not felt and released can result in serious consequences, including chronic illnesses, depression, cancer, and other diseases. Relationships, jobs, and material possessions can momentarily distract us but will never permanently change how we feel about ourselves. Likewise, it is imperative that we manage our emotions. The key to successfully maintaining a healthy lifestyle is discovering both mental (books, music, arts, spiritual reflection) and physical outlets (walking, running, swimming, cycling, dancing) that work for each of us individually.

A. What Are You Really Afraid Of?

Fears are nothing more than a state of mind.
—Napoleon Hill

I AM TRULY AFRAID of snakes and the idea of thieves in the night. But I'm not afraid of mice—okay, maybe rats. I'm also not afraid of being alone or of dying. In fact, although I love this life on the earth and I'm in no hurry to leave it, I can't wait to be in heaven with all the dearly departed, my loved ones who are already there. We're talking about having no more pain or fears and a "glorified body." Well, I don't know exactly what that looks like, but I think it will be awesome.

A very real fear for many of us is coming to terms with our feelings. When ignored, this results in withdrawal and ultimately separates us from others. This mentality of staying detached and living a life in fear so as not to hurt or be hurt by others causes much of the isolation and loneliness in the world today. If we open ourselves to the truth that every relationship is a gift from God and actually serves a purpose in our life, then we might find it easier to love those we've been blessed to know. However, it is important to distinguish here that if a relationship feels abusive in any way (mentally, physically, or emotionally) and if there is no hope of changed behavior, then we must protect and take care of ourselves by removing ourselves from that person or situation.

Why would God give us feelings as well as sight, touch, taste, and smell if we weren't meant to feel? Our feelings are real and there for a reason. This is a perfect example of when we need to listen to that sixth sense, otherwise known as our gut feeling. Mothers, being completely responsible for another human being, seem to be the best at tapping into this gut feeling. And if we ignore our feelings and automatic responses to everyday stimuli, we will eventually lose the ability to effectively manage those feelings and behaviors. Shutting down any one of our senses authenticates the viewpoint that "if we don't use it, we're going to lose it." The best way to overcome fears is to face them, and for me, this usually involves awareness and education. Many times, I don't have all the facts, and my fears are simply of the unknown. Once I've educated myself to the best of my ability, I'm willing, ready, and able to face any fears I might have had.

Likewise, we must take ourselves outside our comfort zone and put ourselves in situations where we will have to deal with our fears. For each one of us, the fears that we have been programmed with are due to our own life experiences and will vary drastically. Even within our own family of origin, we will not necessarily develop the same fears. The role we have played in our family, as well as the subsequent responses and reactions received from family members, will influence and affect the development of fears and eventually insecurities in our life.

As I continue to reflect on fear, I am reminded that there is always an appropriate time and place for our feelings. So before I am misunderstood or my thoughts are misconstrued, I just want to say that self-control—along with a peaceful surrender to the reality of one's feelings—will result in an acceptable manner of processed feelings. Many times, I need to give myself time to process feelings before I respond. If I don't, I am apt to put my foot in my mouth and potentially say or do something that I later regret or wish I have said or done a little differently.

Because I'm pretty open and honest, I've been told that I'm one of those people whose feelings most everyone knows. Well, this may seem true; but in reality, there are so many more times when we keep our feelings inside, myself included, in fear of making someone else angry or disappointed in us. So I guess you could say that we're more afraid of someone else's feelings. Hmm, in all honesty, I have to admit I do think God has given me an extra dose of feelings. Many times, I not only feel my own feelings but also feel someone else's. I tear up just thinking about the pain or suffering someone else is going through. This empathy has taught me to pray for God's will not only for myself but also for others. Surely then, empathy, compassion, and prayers are the greatest blessings we can give to one another. If we truly trust God, then we can live in the peace, joy, and hope of knowing and trusting that—like any great father—God knows what is best for all His children.

In conclusion, I'd like to add that I am a very strong advocate of finding healthy choices in tackling our fears. As I have said, for me, researching and educating myself on whatever it is that I am hesitant or fearful about has always been the key to processing and eventually overcoming the fears, challenges, and struggles life throws at me. In addition, I truly believe that in sharing our feelings with trusted and respected people, we obtain a better perspective, as well as a healthy response (rather than reaction) to conflicted or misunderstood feelings.

B. All Dogs (Don't) Go to Heaven . . . but Weezy Did!

*It is amazing how much love and laughter they bring
into our lives and even how much closer we become with
each other because of them.*

—John Grogan

FOR THOSE WHO are not familiar with this movie, *All Dogs Go to Heaven* is an animated musical fantasy comedy-drama film released by United Artists in 1989. Not knowing how heavy this animated film was, I took my boys to this movie about dogs when they were six and four, hoping afterward that they were too young to absorb the darkness in the story line. I thought it would be a good life lesson, especially if the dogs put a fun spin on the message of going to heaven. But in the movie, only the good and obedient dogs went to heaven, not exactly the message our loving and forgiving Father gave us through His Son.

Anyone who has ever had a dog knows that they love unconditionally just as our Father does. That being said, I must say that I have always enjoyed the company of a good dog. The following reflection on the cutest pug ever, Weezy, is yet another example of me processing my feelings by expressing them in writing.

After a family visit to Tarpon Springs, Florida, over the Christmas holidays with the next year's college plans intact, my eldest son, Bobby, took a winter-term job on his senior year of high school in a pet store. Always the dog lover, he was thrilled to be around dogs and others who shared his passion, even if it meant doing what no one else liked to do. Cleaning up after the dogs was one of his first duties, and we all know how dreary that can be.

I am a firm believer that owning a family dog is a great opportunity for learning what it's like to care for and take accountability for someone or something else other than ourselves. Equally notable is the fact that small children and dogs visit retirement homes. They not only bring life and laughter into our homes but they are darn good company too.

Our family has enjoyed many pets over the years, but our first choice has always been a dog. Our first family dog of twelve years, a Shih Tzu named Taffy was much more of a mommy's girl but certainly spent time curled up on everyone's lap or bed, including my middle son, Jimbo. For some reason, although he never really encouraged her, Taffy would sit outside his bedroom door wanting to go in for a nap. As for Haylee, what Taffy has loved to do in my precious daughter's room is another story altogether, and I'll save that one for another time.

How Weezy joined the family is the story to share. One afternoon, I received an excited call from Bobby about a pug that had just arrived in the pet store. According to Bobby, he was the best dog that had ever come into the store, and I must come over and see him right away. Two hours later, I left the pet store with the most adorable and loving pug I had ever seen.

Weezy became a part of the family and a legend in his own right over the next decade. He loved everyone and went everywhere with us. He was photographed a thousand times over. You see, to meet Weezy was to love him. He had the longest tongue in the history of pugs, and his sweet temperament allowed him to never take a bad picture.

Once while taking a walk with Weezy in the Centennial Park in Nashville, Tennessee, a professional photographer asked if he could take just a few pictures of Weezy. Let's just say that, an hour later, the photographer had more than a few pictures to choose from. Truth be told, the picture I took of Haylee and Weezy that very same day continues to be the picture that appears whenever my Haylee girl calls.

I would have never guessed that less than twenty-four hours after I left home for Tarpon Springs for the first time in thirteen years for the Christmas holidays, Weezy would die just shy of his thirteenth birthday. But then I realized once again it was just as it should be. Although Weezy's health had been declining all year, he wouldn't die until I left the house because that was what our beloved pets would do. Weezy would be forever remembered and missed by our family but most especially by his partner in crime, Aubrie, who came all the way from Auburn to live and play with Weezy.

Aubrie is another "Bobby" dog story. Bobby rescued Aubrie during his senior year in college. She grew up around Bobby and his friends, never a dull moment, bless her heart. Once Bobby graduated and began working full time, he was concerned that Aubrie was spending too much time at home alone. Likewise, he began bringing Aubrie girl over to the house for play dates with Weezy, first during the day and then weekends. Upon returning from a fishing trip to Florida, Bobby came by the house to pick sweet Aubrie girl up, and she just didn't want to leave Weezy; and as they'd say, the rest was history. Aubrie lived on another three years after Weezy died, finally enjoying her status as queen of the house until she too passed.

My heartfelt thanks goes out to my eldest son, who has always had the same passion for dogs that I have, for bringing sweet Weezy and Aubrie into our lives. They are probably all playing together in heaven right now.

C. If You Don't Laugh, You Just Might Cry

It's better to cry than be angry, because anger hurts others while tears flow silently through the soul and cleanse the heart.

—Pope John Paul II

"TEARS SILENTLY FLOWING through the soul, cleansing the heart"—what a beautiful thought Pope John Paul has given us to ponder! Crying is, indeed, a healthy and cleansing expression of feelings. For me, tears come so naturally when I am truly touched, especially when I witness love being expressed toward one another. And just as easily, when I'm under pain or stress, springs of water well up in me, flowing freely, cleansing my heart. I simply can't stop the flow. I'm truly like a leaky faucet. The good news is, as I process my feelings and the tears flow, I begin the healing process.

The most obvious example of this is the death of my beloved firstborn, Bobby. When I think of him and how much I miss him, my tears flow ever so freely, even now as I type these words. But I know he is living in heaven in peace with all our dearly departed, and a hopeful smile breaks through my sadness. Again, there are tears with the news of my daughter, Haylee, and her family moving across country to Bend, Oregon. I have cried just thinking about how different life will be. And don't even get me started on the two little boys whom Haylee and Mike have chosen to bring into this world. They have brought so much joy into our lives over the past five years. Their births have been a gift to us all and, as always, perfectly timed. But once again, witnessing the beautiful life they are living on a five-acre farmhouse has replaced my tears with peace and joy for the whole family.

Anger can be both an easy and hard feeling to draw on. Sometimes it truly is easier to be mad than sad. However, as Pope John Paul states, anger is much more likely to produce more hurt feelings and ultimately causes situations to get worse long before they get better. Additionally, anger taken out on another human being always seems, to me, to be a waste of time and energy. I always feel mentally and physically exhausted if I do let anger get the best of me.

However, when used constructively, frustration or anger can be an effective motivator. When someone or something stirs anger in me, many times, it inspires me to get the job done. Especially if I've been told I can't do something, my mentality becomes "watch me." The most explicit example of this that I can think of is when I was told twenty years ago that I could not build a pool in my sloping backyard. Six estimates later and a crash course in architectural design, I have a beautiful backyard with pool, truly what I like to call a little piece of paradise. Bottom line, I think there is constructive and destructive behavior that results from anger; but in any case, the feeling is real, and it certainly needs to be processed as quickly and effectively as possible.

Okay, so there are times when we need to cry; and again, we need to be angry, but let's not forget to partake of one of the greatest feelings of all—joy. In other words, enjoy a good laugh as often as possible. Sometimes we laugh at others; sometimes we laugh at ourselves. I seem to get the biggest kick out of enjoying myself when the joke is on me. It's not to say I set myself up to be laughed at. No, not at all. Many times when I'm laughing at myself, no one else is even present. That being said, if there *are* only two emotions and they are rooted in love or fear, then when I'm laughing with myself, I'm also loving myself. If I'm afraid to laugh at myself, then insecurities—false or real—have gotten the best of me.

As a child my mom told me it would always behoove me to be somewhere in the middle when expressing my feelings at school. She advised me to never be the first and never be the last. For this reason, I rarely was the one to get in trouble when the whole class was inappropriately laughing because I was aware of my surroundings and knew when to stop. I felt that it was a really good advice, and I love her endlessly for all the beautiful wisdom she shared with me.

As for talking, well, let's just say that would be another story—it would take a whole lot more discipline for me to stop talking. My fourth-grade teacher, Mrs. Jones, signed my yearbook "To my talker." I give her credit for bringing me out of my shell. She was one of those teachers you never forget. She not only was an awesome instructor who had fun with her class but she also brought out the best in her students. My mom said that I had always been a quiet, timid little girl who rarely expressed her feelings, especially in public; but during that year, I grew in confidence and poise. At the same time, my little personality was coming to life, and it stuck with me.

"There she goes, cracking herself up again." At least that's what my kids might say. And if that's what they decide to put on my tombstone, I'm okay with that too. I've never really had a problem with being vulnerable enough to show my feelings. So for me, that includes laughing as well as crying. If I'm touched by the moment, whether in real life or, say, with a movie, then I cry. If I'm tickled pink or humored by something or someone else, then I have no qualms about laughing out loud. Again, feelings are good and need to be processed and expressed, but I also have to reiterate here that timely expressions of our feelings are of utmost importance. Appropriately, this reflects a sensitivity to others' feelings as well as our own. "It's never all about me," and the sooner we realize this, the sooner we mature.

D. You Want Me to Do What? Express Myself?

You are an artist of the spirit. Find yourself and express yourself in your own particular way. Express your love openly. Life is nothing but a dream, and if you create your life with love, your dream becomes a masterpiece of art.
—Don Miguel Ruiz

F OR MANY YEARS, I have come to realize that I come to life when I am surrounded by the truth and beauty of the arts. Art, music, and dance as well as the written word move me into seeing, hearing, and feeling a beautiful existence around me that God has created to nurture my mind, body, and soul. It doesn't take long to look around and see, hear, and feel the brokenness of the world, but we can be quickly transformed with thoughtful reflection on all the goodness that also surrounds us. My life is a reflection of what I focus on each day, and I choose to focus on the truth, the good, and the beautiful.

There are so many ways to express ourselves. Art, music, dance, photography, style, fashion, and the culinary arts are just a few that come to mind. I believe we have been created with a very basic need to express ourselves and have been doing so since the beginning of time. The arts not only stimulate our thoughts, ideas, and emotions but they also provide a vehicle to express and communicate them. It occurs to me that this need for expressing ourselves is also the ultimate way of processing our feelings. Whether it's a book, a work of art, a dance, or a song, the feelings and emotions felt by the author, artist, dancer, or musician at that moment are most undeniably revealed. These gifts of expression become something we have created, and likewise, our talents are noted and appreciated as we add beauty to the world around us.

The first expression that comes to my mind is our freedom of speech in America. We are free to express ourselves verbally as well as in the written word. I don't usually have a problem expressing myself, but truth be told, there are many times when I don't share how I think or feel about a person or situation. Sometimes it's simply because I feel like enough has already been said by others. And other times, I don't really have a direct experience or an emotional attachment, and so my feelings don't seem strong enough to participate in a debate or heated verbal exchange. Then there are those other times when I get really excited about what's being discussed and become completely engaged and excited about entering into the discussion.

But when the dust has settled and I make the time, I usually turn to expressing myself in the written word. It is so freeing and has always been a kind of therapy for me. There's no rushing, no loud voices, no distractions, and I'm able to peacefully collect and process my thoughts. If my mind is distracted or I just can't seem to focus, I will generally read something factual or inspirational pertaining to what's on my mind and then go from there. Once I'm engaged, I get lost in the discussion, completely unaware of the passing of time. Okay, so that works for me but not for you. Let's go back to the list.

Many times, the words of a song or hymn reflect exactly what is in our head that hasn't been put into words. I've heard it said that when you sing a hymn, you're actually praying twice. Although very much an amateur myself, music really does move my soul. There are times when I am singing with the Life Teen band at our church and simply have to stop and lip-synch because the words of the song are stirring my emotions so much that my voice has begun to tremble. What a smack of reality—I have lost my voice because I have found my emotion.

I'd never forget the recital when Haylee, only about fourteen at the time, sang "God Help the Outcasts" from Walt Disney's *The Hunchback of Notre Dame*. Although I'd heard her sing the song several times during lessons, when I heard her sing it at the recital, it was as if I had just heard it for the first time, and I couldn't stop the tears from flowing. And of course, I didn't have any Kleenex; so by the time the song was sung, my pant legs were wet from wiping my tears on them. I was sure the rest of the family thought I was nuts.

Another time I had been moved to tears with music was listening to a beautiful instrumental song, "The Battle," composed by Jimmy, my middle son. He wrote and dedicated this song to his late brother, and for years, I couldn't listen to him play it without tearing up. It was so beautifully reflective, and it didn't even have words; it was all about the music.

Yet for others, the easiest and most natural form of expression comes through some type of physical outlet such as a sport, dance, or martial arts. Although a nonverbal communication, thoughts and feelings can be expressed just as effectively with body movement. Walking and running have not only become a popular form of exercise in recent years but also been noted as an effective therapy. It has become a sought-after time for many to unwind, reflect, or regroup.

There truly is so much truth and beauty in the arts. It's an absolutely awe-inspiring gift of personal expression to the world, as well as a healthy and productive way to understand, make sense of, and deal with our emotions.

CHAPTER IV

Honoring Relationships

If you want a relationship that looks and feels like the most amazing thing on earth, you need to treat it like it is the most amazing thing on earth.

—Intentional Today

OUR STORIES ARE as unique and special as we are, and they are formed by our family of origin as well as our life experiences in our home and community. We might all well be created equal, but our formation can be as different as night is from day. In light of this, when we make the decision to enter into relationships, we have to remember that any important relationship requires love and grace. No two people have the same story, and both are of equal value to the relationship. We have to continuously give thanks and appreciation for every relationship we are blessed to receive. Real relationships take work, and without attention, care, and service, it is next to impossible to build something as real as an authentic relationship.

It has become trendy to cite research by British anthropologist Robin Dunbar when reflecting on relationships. Dunbar's number, as it is called, suggests that people can effectively manage about 150 relationships. That seems to me like a lot of relationships. The good news is the number of relationships we actually attend to will drastically differ for each person. The challenging news is no matter how many or how deeply we are involved, all relationships take hard work.

So what does it look like to effectively manage our relationships? If we acknowledge the fact that real relationships take time and commitment and don't happen overnight, we have to also confess the need to continuously nourish and protect them. Otherwise, they will cease to exist. A common pattern of behavior that exists in all authentic relationships is respect. We must give respect to receive it, and no matter how big our differences are, we have to constantly remind ourselves that everyone deserves respect. To respect a person is to understand that the person is *not* us—not an extension, not a reflection, and not a product of us. Respect, including responsibility and accountability to each other, results in a safe and approachable atmosphere that creates lasting trust, confidence, and hope in the relationship.

In a relationship of respect, our task is to accept and understand each other as the unique individuals we have been created to be. Love without respect is dangerous and can crush the spirit of another person. Our task is *not* to change or control another person in a direction we desire but to love and appreciate them for who they are. With continued and consistent respect for each other, trust ultimately follows.

When a relationship isn't centered on mutual respect, trust, and love for each other, irreconcilable differences occur. Whatever connection has existed is severed, and the relationship eventually dissipates. When the scales are tipped in a relationship and mutually respectful behavior doesn't exist, a constant power struggle develops in an effort to restore the equality that is pertinent to all authentic relationships.

Again, I am reminded of the instructive and fruitful philosophy of our forefathers of America that we have all been created equal and deserve to be treated as such. Adhering to this philosophy does, in fact, preserve and protect life, liberty, and the pursuit of happiness. A key element to note here is that this philosophy has to be practiced in our homes and communities long before we can ever expect it to be followed around the world.

A. The Importance of Attraction, Chemistry, Family, and Faith

The important thing is not to think much but to love much; and so do that which best stirs you to love.
—St. Teresa of Avila

LET'S START WITH the importance of attraction and chemistry in a relationship. Remember those feelings that simply take over when we are attracted to someone of the opposite sex—butterflies in our stomach, rapid and shallow breathing, weakness, light-headedness, can't eat, can't sleep, can't focus. These twitterpated feelings that take over our mind, body, and soul when we think we have met that special someone are real. The truth of the matter is that all lasting relationships are built and thrive on a connection that comes from within and brings people together for a season or a lifetime. This certainly is a recurring theme in life, isn't it?

This leads us to the importance of family and lifestyle. Whether we like it or not, a simple reality of life is that our family and friends have had a major influence on us since the day we were born. Our belief system, our likes and dislikes, and our social, political, and economical views all originate from our loved ones. Now once we begin our adult formation, we may alter or even change our way of thinking, but we can never deny its origin. Our lifestyle reflects all these influences, past and present. Likewise, the way we manage our relationships will, at least initially, be patterned much after our parents and grandparents as well as close family friends. Consequently, even if we're attracted to someone but we don't have a common interest in sharing our lives with each other in relationship, we will quickly become detached and pursue our personal interests. So when we are blessed to be in a genuine and connected relationship, we must both be intentional and deliberate about investing time and energy in the relationship. Time spent together will ultimately reveal if the relationship is superficial and temporary or sincere and permanent.

And last but certainly not least in our discernment is our faith. I believe our faith is at the very core of our soul, and without it, we don't share the common denominator that keeps us together forever. When we believe in the sanctification of our relationship, we share a sense of purpose and connection that goes way beyond shared careers, interests, or hobbies. Likewise, when we feel uncomfortable sharing our spiritual beliefs and experiences, we may struggle to stay connected in a relationship. And while many beliefs and ideas may vary from person to person, without a spiritual connection, relationships don't have the necessary pool of resources to draw from during times of stress or conflict. When faith is the cornerstone, a relationship has something to stand on and will continue to grow and mature. Without a common faith, respect, and trust in a person, we can't possibly expect to build on all the other pertinent components of a relationship that give it strength and durability in the good and bad times.

Relationships centered in God just naturally evolve, and likewise, joy, peace, and happiness come from that union. A relationship should never be forced or controlled. When it is, it is because there isn't a mutual desire to be in the relationship. We never want to be with that person who takes relationships for granted or thinks they are difficult or too much hard work. Rather, what we hope for is being with someone who recognizes and appreciates that the relationship is truly a privilege and a gift from God. With that understanding, we are ready to give and receive all that life, love, and God have to offer. With the attraction and chemistry that has first brought us together and a united belief system of what God and family mean to us, we first become friends and then lovers in an integrated relationship that lasts a lifetime.

One of the most meaningful songs ever written about what it looks like to be a true friend in a relationship centered in God is "Friends," written by the Christian singer and songwriter Michael W. Smith. He has written in the chorus of the song, "And friends are friends forever if the Lord's the Lord of them. And a friend will not say 'never' 'cause the welcome will not end. Though it's hard to let you go, in the Father's hands we know that a lifetime's not too long to live as friends." These lyrics reflect the sincerity of a lasting relationship. Whether we're facing a new chapter in life—a new job, a move across the country, or even death—a true friendship remains constant and bears distance and even adversity. We accept each right where we are and are happy for each other even when it hurts. And then no matter how long it's been between visits, we pick up right where we left off.

B. What's My Role?

A great relationship doesn't happen because of the love you had in the beginning but how well you continue building love until the end.

—Anonymous

A PERSON'S ROLE IN any relationship is that which has developed and been agreed on by the people in it. So although the role we played in our family of origin becomes a dominant factor in our personal and social interaction with others, it doesn't necessarily have to be played out in every relationship thereafter. Birth order as well as the personality types of our parents and siblings will all play a major role in our development, but as mature and healthy adults, we learn to build on our own strengths. The good news is that, today, we don't have to worry about what is or isn't traditional or acceptable; we get to figure that out for ourselves. A very wise person (my mother) told me that, just as with everything else in life, not everything in a relationship is always fair; but the sooner I accept and let go of whatever it is that seems to be unfair, the better.

Growing up, I indeed felt the love and acceptance of my family. Be that as it may, my role in the family was to be the good and responsible one; and honestly speaking, who wouldn't love that family member? In the midst of growing up around an elder sibling who loved to do things her way and certainly wasn't ever afraid of the consequences, I became the person who didn't want to rock the boat or cause any more anxiety or grief for my parents. Likewise, I succumbed to not really expressing my needs or desires in subsequent relationships as well. And as a result, I never thought of mine as a priority and certainly never more important.

Although you won't hear me complaining, I have to admit that this idea that we have all played a very specific role in our immediate family leaves me a little hungry for what's next. Whatever the need or pecking order described in previous relationships has been, I think it is wise that we open ourselves up to other possibilities, new information, and further development of our adult personality and lifestyle. With an open mind, we allow ourselves to take the good and change the bad, otherwise known as accountability and responsibility. Ah, the wisdom and maturity that comes with age.

As a young wife and mother of three, I carried "my role" into my little family, still desiring to do whatever I deemed necessary to make everyone else happy. Many times, I gave up doing or going where I wanted just to be with my family. But don't get me wrong, that was exactly where I wanted to be. Being a part of their lives and making them happy made me happy. The unconditional sacrifices and selflessness of a young mother are very genuine and real and can never be denied; however, neither can the gifts of love, appreciation, and gratitude that are received in exchange.

As a mature woman, I realize that our feelings and needs are of equal value; and when denied over a long period, an imbalance and inequality can be created in any relationship. Whenever a relationship shifts out of balance, we feel unsafe and experience insecure feelings of hurt, anger, unfairness, betrayal, and mistrust. There will be times when one person's needs are more pressing, but the important thing to remember is that, out of respect and kindness, we need to take turns in the relationship, and we need to both be there for each other. As life unfolds, our needs and desires will inevitably change, and the key to the success of any healthy relationship is the flexibility to accept and change with them. So actually, our role is to maintain a balance in all our relationships, whether they be personal or professional, casual or romantic.

Finding this balance can be difficult, especially since we are taught by platforms like social media and gender socialization that some kind of power dynamic is the norm in any relationship. There are several elements (love, honor, respect, and desire) needed to create a balanced relationship in which both parties feel safe. It is our responsibility to love and honor ourselves first and then others. We have to take our wants and needs seriously and give them the respect they deserve so that what we have to offer is not only for a relationship but also for the whole world. Only when both people know their own strengths and weaknesses can we create balance in a relationship. This balance is noted, respected, and desired by others.

When imbalanced, we are not listening to either our own thoughts, feelings, and interests or those of another person. By focusing on both, we can't help but want to support and care for them. When we treat each other with love and respect, we feel safe and secure in the relationship knowing that each of our needs and desires are being met. And the more we appreciate and honor each other, the stronger the relationship becomes. Our role becomes that of a personal investment in the relationship, a mutual responsibility and accountability to the success of the relationship, the family, the community, and so on.

C. Why Not Give Love a Chance?

Be yourself. Everyone else is taken.

—Oscar Wilde

PEOPLE COME IN and out of our lives every day, but true love and lasting relationships are a gift from God and don't come along as often. So what's holding us back? Why is more than half the population afraid of commitment? It is a proven fact that healthy relationships improve all aspects of life, strengthening our mind, body, and soul. However, it is also true that relationships that aren't working can tremendously drain us and negatively affect all areas of life. So what's the missing link? Why not give love a chance?

From a very young age, we're told, "The more we put into it, the more we get out of it." Well, that certainly holds true for relationships. Strong, healthy relationships are one of the best support systems we have available. Mutually respectful relationships are an investment in our joy, peace, and happiness today as well as in the future. Just as good relationships should never be ignored or neglected, they should never be rushed or forced either as time has a way of revealing all things. And as hard and lonely as being single can sometimes seem, when we're in a relationship with the wrong person, we can feel even more alone and unhappier.

This is why it is so important to make sure the person we choose to fall in love with is someone who loves the way we laugh and will do absolutely anything to hear it, knows our favorite color as well as our favorite pastime, is anxious to share with us everything important in life, will never want to frustrate or hurt us, considers our feelings in every choice, can't wait to introduce us to every person in their life, can't wait to hug and kiss us each and every time they see us, thinks that we are the one person in the whole world that they want to see every night before they go to bed and every morning before they rise, and is the one person in the whole world we simply cannot live without. Is this idealistic or the thoughts of a dreamer? I don't think so.

It is very important to begin each and every relationship being completely open and honest. If either of us is trying to be anyone other than ourselves, it's only a matter of time before the real person is revealed. So when we entertain the idea of establishing a new relationship, why not be ourselves? Okay, so let's think about how we will react the next time we are introduced to someone who seems to have all the qualities of a person we like to be in a relationship with. What do we do, and how do we start a qualified conversation that allows us to actually get to know each other? Well, let's start with what's really important to us. A beginning conversation might include the following question: What are three things I should know about you and you should know about me?

If I'm suggesting that open and honest communication is the best policy for all relationships, then let it begin with me. My response to this question is as follows:

1. If you are truly interested in a committed relationship with me, you need to know that the Catholic faith, which I feel so blessed to have been born into, is at the core of my very soul. I would like to share one faith because I believe that a relationship centered on God is a loving and lasting one. In my experience, this cannot be compromised, or the relationship will not be a long-lasting one.
2. I love and adore my family and lifelong friends, and I will never compromise the relationship I have with them. I strongly believe a relationship needs to be nourished, protected, and made top priority, but it will need to be supportive and inclusive of my immediate family, whom I love with my whole heart.
3. I am open and willing to explore the idea of marriage but will never rush into it. I think people need to get to know each other and spend quality time together, allowing a relationship to unfold and grow naturally and authentically.

Strong, healthy long-term relationships don't happen overnight. They take awareness, commitment, perseverance, and a definite sense of being present. If communication *is* the key to every good relationship, and I truly believe it is, then it is also not fair to wait to mention deal breakers in any relationship. We should protect our heart as well as that of others. Also, we ought to keep in mind how the relationship is making us feel. Are we being true to ourselves? Does this person encourage us to be our authentic self? When we have been true to ourselves and have given as much love, time, and energy as we can to ensure that our relationship is something that is satisfying and fulfilling to both of us, it will become increasingly obvious if it is time to peacefully move forward or away from the relationship.

So say yes—give love a chance, but be yourself, be honest and be real, and don't lie about your expectations or deal breakers in a relationship. Kick back, relax, and enjoy the ride, savoring every moment of every day. Life is too short not to.

D. Accepting Life on Life's Terms

Peace is the result of retraining your mind to process
life as it is, rather than as you think it should be.
—Wayne W. Dyer

ACCEPTING LIFE ON life's terms is surely easier said than done. Life and everyone in it is never going to be perfect, but the power of acceptance gives us the much-needed perspective of what we do and do not have control over. Life's challenge then is learning when to accept what has happened, is happening, and will happen as something that is out of our control. The way we process and deal with the people, places, and things that we have no control over holds the key to leading a happier, more serene, and more satisfying life. Are we truly in acceptance or just faking it?

Authentic acceptance means accepting but not necessarily agreeing with that which has or indeed is happening as the reality it is. Once the process of acceptance has begun, a spiritual meaning and even significance can be identified. The profound and wonderful significance resulting from this process is none other than wisdom. Our wisdom grows from the soil of reality, identified, processed, and accepted. With that and time comes the healing necessary to live a life filled with gratitude and not sorrow over which we have no control over anyway.

We each have our own unique challenges, suffering, and pain, and it is our choice to use them to make ourselves a better person or to let them get the best of us. Deciding to live life on life's terms honors the immensity of faith while strengthening our ability to be discerning, all the while deepening our acceptance of all that is out of our control. When grace guides our acceptance, we don't see these things as unfortunate but rather as opportunities for growth and being further informed by all that life has to offer—the good, the bad, the happy, and the sad.

Learning to accept others right where they are is sometimes an overwhelming component of accepting life on life's terms. Equally important, however, is fully accepting ourselves and not letting fear of rejection keep us from being open and honest with our true feelings about ourselves and others. The authentic acceptance of one another is the key to making any relationship a thriving and lasting one. It's so easy to accept those who think and behave as we do, but accepting others who have their own unique set of beliefs and values that are much different from our own can be so hard. How do we accomplish this?

Complete acceptance of other human beings comes with loving one another for who we are without any judgments. It is a relationship filled with love, compassion, empathy, and understanding. When we commit to going the extra mile of fully accepting those with whom we are in a relationship, we give each other one of the greatest gifts ever received, the essence of unconditional love.

It might be worth mentioning here that no one exercises authority. We both do what is necessary in the name of love to protect and honor our relationship. Love and relationships are not just a birthright but also the result of loving attention and dedication to honor the world that each person brings into the relationship. Sometimes that means accepting a pattern of behavior, and sometimes that means learning to accept a change in behavior, doing whatever is possible to foster the relationship. Slight shifts will have a greater impact than major efforts at change and eventually will become the new normal. Acceptance, sincerity, and patience will also give the relationship the depth and strength needed to withstand all the challenges that arise. This concept of authentic acceptance requires a considerable amount of work, and likewise, only those willing to put constant and continual effort into their relationships will achieve it. It is a mutual process, allowing a genuine relationship based on love and trust for one another to evolve naturally.

When we are blessed by authentic acceptance, we don't feel the need to keep our thoughts and emotions locked away. We are free to feel and speak openly and honestly about our life experiences. We are more patient and tolerant. We take a more thoughtful and reflective attitude toward ourselves and others. We are confident in offering our own precious individuality to the relationship, as well as accepting theirs. Anything less results in superficial relationships that don't stand the test of time.

Just the same, I believe every relationship is unique and imperfect, and every relationship serves a purpose. Even when a relationship ends, we can use it as a source of revelation. With the identification that the natural maturing process of becoming a better person has been stunted, the end of the relationship is the mutual setting free of each other so that becoming a better version of oneself is once again attainable. It is the ultimate acceptance of accepting life on life's terms, placing honor and value in doing what is best for all without blame or judgment. In this case, the understanding and appreciation that life and love are a miracle and that we don't have any control over the occurrence or timing of them is the revelation.

CHAPTER V

Enjoying Life

The secret of being happy is accepting where you are in life and making the most out of every day.

WHAT DOES IT mean to enjoy life? Am I allowing life to just happen, or am I making a mindful choice to make each day count? Am I a dynamic participant or a passive bystander?

It is up to us, not anyone else, to find meaning and purpose in our lives. To increase our level of enjoyment, we must be doing our best to consciously engage ourselves by actively listening and responding to our spouse, children, and friends. It really does always come back to the philosophy that it's not the quantity but the quality of the time we spend with one another that counts.

With each season of life, a different set of opportunities as well as challenges arise. Knowing and accepting this to be true, how do we make the most out of every day, every situation? Accepting each day and season with an open mind reminds us that we are not victims of our circumstances but that we are in control of our enjoyment of life at any given time. Being present, being curious, and being ourselves lead us to living a life of simple abundance and one of feeling fully alive. By truly connecting with our authentic self, we give ourselves the opportunity to tap into our uniqueness. Why not be ourselves? Everyone else is already taken.

Many of us play it safe in life, squandering our own precious gifts and talents. Not willing to take creative risks, we continue to compare our talents with others and don't make investments in our true self. Many times, we play it safe for so long that we become miserable and unproductive and understandably have no idea about what has made us this way. Playing it safe can be the riskiest choice we ever make. It's been said that if we don't stand for something, we'll fall for anything. Well, I think the exact same thing is true with exploring dreams and setting goals. If we don't commit to something, we'll be distracted by everything.

This struggle will end once we take an honest look in the mirror to see who we really are. The personal gifts we have received give our unique creative expression to something that might otherwise not exist. No one can take these talents away from us; only we can chose to withhold them from others. When we stop denying our God-given talents and become willing to own them humbly, gratefully, and respectfully, only then are we able to share them with the rest of the world. There is a lot of truth in what Henry Ford said: "To do more for the world than the world does for you—that is success."

A. Are You Living in the Present?

I am living in the present, thinking about the past, hoping for the future.

—Paul Auster

HMM, HOW MANY hours a day are we truly living in the present? Living in the present means that our awareness is completely centered on the here and now. Our mindfulness is actively paying attention to the present. When we live in the present, we are living where life is happening. Our thoughts and actions are intentional. We are not worrying about the future or thinking about the past. Those moments when we are so engrossed in what we're doing that we lose track of time and everything else around us are when we know we are truly living in the present.

In this fast-paced world we live in today, it is imperative that we try really hard to live more fully in the present and enjoy every experience as it presents itself. Our "turned on" world contributes in a major way to distracting us and making us falsely believe that there is always something else that we need to be doing. But when we actively engage our mind, body, and soul in the present, our life and the lives of those around us are enhanced exponentially. Whether we are writing a book or playing with our grandchildren, when we are consciously practicing our awareness in all our actions, we allow ourselves to enjoy the experience to the fullest. Our mind is focused on whatever it is that we are doing, and we are not thinking about the 101 other things we need to do today. We are simply living in the moment.

This awareness cultivates resilience when our minds want to drift off without our permission. By noticing what's happening, we begin to work constructively with the actual events in our lives rather than getting pulled into fearful, angry, or depressing thoughts about fictitious events that may or may not happen. Likewise, our awareness is anchored and produces the kind of impulsivity and reactivity that is creative rather than destructive.

For example, when we are faced with pain and suffering, the mind's natural tendency is to attempt to avoid it. Unfortunately, negative situations and the onset of feelings that occur can't be avoided, and resisting them usually only makes them worse. By letting the emotion be there without trying to change or manipulate the outcome, our acceptance of the way things are relieves us of needless extra suffering. Our acceptance and ability to live in the present without regrets, fears, or doubts is the direct result of having processed our feelings and emotions.

Focusing on the present also keeps us from overthinking. How many times have we overthought a situation, worried about the outcome, only to discover later that it worked itself out? Stephen Schueller, a psychologist at the University of Pennsylvania, states, "Being present-minded takes away some of that self-evaluation and getting lost in your mind—and in the mind is where we make the evaluations that beat us up." What an absolute waste of time and energy!

Not only will living in the present have a dramatic effect on our emotional well-being but it will also affect our physical health. It comes as no surprise that the amount of mental stress we carry will have a detrimental impact on our health. Many situations that happen to and around us put stress on our body. Unchecked, we can dramatically increase this stress with our negative thoughts. When we face continuous challenges without any relief or peace, stress-released tension builds up and affects our body. If we've ever felt stressed, our personal anguish can lead to many physical symptoms, including high blood pressure, chest pains, headache, and stomachache, as well as problems sleeping.

Research suggests that stress and taking drugs and alcohol are much like adding fuel to the fire with disease and chronic illness. Unfortunately, rather than returning the body to a relaxed state in which it can efficiently perform, the body tends to stay in a stressed state, causing even more problems. These symptoms are actually signals of the much deeper impact that stress can have on every organ and system in our body, from the muscular and digestive systems to the circulatory and immune systems. The good news is when we remain in the present and actively engage in a healthy lifestyle, we can successfully manage the effect that stress has on us.

We need to remember that focusing on the good, and not the bad, is a choice and a present we give ourselves. If we're living in the present, we're living in acceptance. If we accept life as it is now, not as how we wish it could have been or will be, we realize everything is exactly as it should be. Time and time again, life proves that we are right where we are supposed to be, and it is up to us to make a conscious and active choice to make the most or the least of every moment. By making a cognizant effort to be fully invested and appreciative of who and what life presents us each day, we allow ourselves to live life to the fullest, enjoying every moment of every day.

B. Dance like Nobody's Watching

Dance like nobody's watching; love like you've never been hurt. Sing like nobody's listening; live like it's heaven on earth.

—Mark Twain

AS I'VE SAID before, I come to life when I am surrounded by the truth and beauty of the arts, especially music and dance. For the past several years, I have been blessed with the opportunity of engaging in ballroom dancing. It has been something I wanted to do for as long as I can remember. And today I simply can't get enough.

It all started during a Fully Alive workshop that I hosted on the state of happiness. We discussed in detail the fact that when our core needs are met, we are happier people. To be more specific, our quality of life is enhanced when we take care of our basic human needs; and likewise, we feel the love, joy, and peace of a good life.

During the workshop, we were asked to determine our current state of happiness based on a "wheel of life" with all aspects of life, including physical, mental, intellectual, and spiritual. On a scale of one to ten, we rated our happiness in each of the following categories: health, family, love and romance, personal growth, finances, and fun and recreation. What I discovered was that, although I was taking care of myself in pretty much all the other categories, I really didn't have anything to add to the category of fun and recreation. And so I gave myself a big fat zero; turned to my best friend, Dianna; and said, "I'm ready to start those ballroom dancing classes I've been talking about. Are you in or out?" And we began our lessons the following week.

I have discovered that dancing isn't just about the steps and music. It's also the perfect combination of physical, mental, and social stimulation. Ballroom dancing is a creative movement that enhances our mind, body, and soul. It improves not only our health and fitness but also our mental sharpness. Studies have shown that dancing contributes to self-discovery, self-confidence, and self-expression. In addition, dancing is a physical release and, as a result, reduces stress and tension.

As a mentor has once said, "Once you learn something, it stays with you forever." Well, I have danced most of my life, taking lessons and being on dance teams throughout school and college, and I'm here to tell you that learning ballroom dance isn't easy. And I sure hope it does stay with me forever.

I honestly feel that music and dance are two things we can do until the day we die. But just as with learning a new language, dancing requires the mind to receive, process, and regurgitate. Dancers evolve each and every week, allowing the mind and body to progressively create from an improved place. We have all witnessed and maybe even tried the newest fitness fads, but ballroom dance is a place where the participant can continue to develop their flexibility, balance, and strength. Posture and confidence will improve, and uncomfortable awkwardness will be replaced with grace and poise. I am a firm believer that the personal values and self-worth that dance produces can remain with us for a lifetime.

Ballroom dancing also helps create a healthy lifestyle. It fosters respect, cooperation, harmony, and confidence as well as a sense of joy, accomplishment, and achievement. The traditional roles of a man and woman interacting and creating beautiful movement together are reinforced while encouraging and protecting the art of conventional ballroom dance.

So what is conventional ballroom dance, and when did it all begin? Ballroom dancing dates back to the sixteenth century, when dances have been held in the royal courts. The American-style ballroom dancing as we know it today falls into two categories: smooth and rhythm. Smooth dances are characterized by elegant, graceful flowing movements covering large areas of the floor with grace and ease, while rhythm dances are almost the opposite in that the goal is to accentuate the percussion of the music with your body in a relatively small space on the floor. In America, the most popular smooth dances are fox-trot, waltz, and tango while the most popular rhythm dances are cha-cha, rumba, and swing. These six dances are a great place to start for any social or competitive dancer.

I myself wanted to be able to dance in both categories, so I initially divided my lessons in half, giving both smooth and rhythm equal attention. It only took me a couple of years to decide that I wanted to try my hand (and foot) at the world of competitive ballroom dancing.

In the past few years, I have been in several organized dance competitions. Each dance experience is unique, each unforgettable. Like every new adventure, there are times when I am very happy with my ballroom dance progress; and other times, I feel like I'm not improving as quickly as I'd like to. All in all, I've been very satisfied and continue to be motivated by ballroom dancing. I'll say, like everything else in life, you get out of it what you put into it. So what am I going to do about it? Practice, practice, and more practice.

C. Putting All the Pieces Together

Learn from yesterday, live for today, hope for tomorrow.
—Anonymous

SO HOW DO we put all the pieces together so that we become the best version of ourselves? No doubt our best chance for living a long and happy life is to remain grateful, avoid unhealthy foods and stressful environments, and stay active. With so many diverse choices today, there really isn't a valid excuse for not making healthy food choices or for not living an active lifestyle in some way, shape, or form. Avoiding stress—well, what can I say? That can sometimes be a little more difficult and certainly seem to be completely out of our control, but in reality, we have a choice in most all things, except life and death.

For me, one of my all-time favorite physical activities is walking. I can walk anywhere, anytime, and I always feel reenergized and ready for whatever the day has in store for me after my morning walk. Next on my personal list is Pilates, a physical fitness system that improves flexibility, increases muscle strength and tone, and develops control and endurance in the entire body. Developed by Joseph Pilates, he and his wife, Clara, opened their first studio in New York City after immigrating to the United States from Germany around 1925. One of Joseph Pilates's students, Carola Strauss Trier, has said in referring to the Pilates method, "Your work is a must. To every human who wants to feel well, stay healthy and be useful." I wholeheartedly agree with Ms. Trier.

I have been going to Pilates classes with Dr. Kimo Kimura of Perfect Health Wellness Center & Pilates Studio here in Atlanta for over twenty years, and I couldn't imagine my life without it. I am as strong and healthy as I've ever been, and I feel like I have the physical and mental endurance to tackle whatever life throws me. Thank you, God. Dr. Kimo is a wealth of information and an avid teacher, sharing absolutely everything he knows about health and wellness with enthusiasm and expertise. However, it is his passion for life that will bring you back to the studio every time.

Constantly encouraging his students to be grateful and to live life to the fullest, he states, "If we're not curious and don't ask questions, we're going to miss out on all the aha moments in life." He persistently suggests that when we take the time to invest in our personal growth opportunities by continuing to discover what it takes for each of us to be stimulated, motivated, fulfilled, and satisfied in life, we will grow a little every day for the rest of our lives.

Again, reminding us that living a full life is a full-body experience, Dr. Kimo concurs that it's not just physical, mental, intellectual, or spiritual but it is also a combination of all parts of the human person. These parts are continuously and constantly interconnected, each part affecting the other. There are no exceptions. We may ignore and even neglect one piece or another, sometimes for extended periods, but not without consequences. Putting all the pieces together includes stimulating, nourishing, and protecting all the pieces. He states, "While our body generally seems to take care of us for the first fifty years, it's up to us to take care of it after the age of fifty." For the most part, this can be done if we take just twenty to thirty minutes a day to address our physical, mental, intellectual, and spiritual needs. Some days, we might be able to invest more, other days less, but the key is consistently devoting our time, energy, and effort toward all aspects of life. Dr. Kimo reminds us that while it may take 30 to 365 days to form a good habit, it only takes 1 day to lose it.

Life is what you make it, so make the best of it. Dr. Kimo promotes enjoying each day to the fullest, taking time for a Kodak moment, and truly giving thanks to those responsible for the person we are today, as the result of being a part of our life. Our happiness and ultimate enjoyment of life is a reflection of our day-to-day attitude and activity— in other words, our lifestyle. We need to surround ourselves with people who understand and appreciate us, and fill our day with opportunities that allow us to grow.

We sometimes falsely believe that happiness is the destination wherein there is no more challenge. In fact, the opposite is true. We thrive and grow off challenge. As Ueshiba Morihei has stated, "Life is growth. If we stop growing, technically and spiritually, we are as good as dead." In just the same way that a Pilates workout can be grueling and painful to someone who is out of shape, our emotional state decides whether the process of being challenged is enjoyable or insurmountable. "We hold our abs in, neck up, back straight; float our bones; and press on." Right, Kimo?

Admittedly, Dr. Kimo states, "Each of us has a different life puzzle, and pulling all the pieces together is a lifelong process, but our awareness and acceptance of the realities of life will actually empower us." A greater personal clarity will consequently give us greater self-worth and allow us to live each day with greater conviction and enthusiasm. Being fully aware and engaged in our surroundings and being conscious all the time will help culminate a dramatic and exciting outlook on life, which is actually one of the first things you can't help but notice about Dr. Kimo and his approach to sharing life with others.

D. What Does It Mean to Be Fully Alive?

The glory of God is man fully alive, and the life of man is the vision of God. If the revelation of God through creation already brings life to all living beings on the earth, how much more will the manifestation of the Father by the Word bring life to those who see God.

—St. Irenaeus

WE TALK ABOUT being fully alive, but what exactly does that mean? I ardently believe that keeping a healthy balance of physical, mental, and spiritual activity in our lives will bring meaning and fullness to all our experiences. Being conscious and aware of ourselves, God, and others keeps us in the here and now, where full life is attainable. It is with the union of our strengths and weaknesses, our joys and sufferings that hope, peace, and joy for each moment become a reality. Being fully alive includes slowing down long enough to smell the roses, listening to the sounds of children playing, and looking up at the sky above in awe and wonder.

To be fully alive means we are open to the whole human experience daily. We are also willing and able to experience the whole gamut of human feelings and emotions. We accept the good with the bad, the happy with the sad. We don't run away from people or situations. We dive into them with the understanding that by collaborating and sharing with others, each experience becomes an opportunity for growth and maturity. We fully embrace the challenges along with the pleasures and look for opportunities to share our life with others.

Then why do so many of us feel lonely, depressed, or unfulfilled? In this upside-down world that we live in today, is it possible that we're simply not taking care of ourselves? Are we going through the motions of life, living each day in a monotonous comfort zone? And worse than that, when nothing eventful is happening to or around us, do we think everything is just fine? Unfortunately, our existence can become stagnant without stimulation and real-life adventures to look forward to. Many times, we become lonely, or we isolate ourselves from others.

If we take a thoughtful and careful look around us, we will see that those people who show signs of life are actively engaged in others and are constantly seeking new ways to motivate and improve themselves. I think Saint Teresa of Calcutta put it best when she has said, "Life is not measured by the number of breaths we take but by the moments that take our breath away."

We have been created to live a life knowing that we are loved and that our lives have purpose and meaning. To some, this may sound too good to be true or unrealistic. But I don't think so. I believe that being fully alive means living in the fruits of the Holy Spirit every day of our life. What are these fruits I'm talking about? Love, joy, peace, patience, kindness, gentleness, generosity, faithfulness, and self-control. Can anyone honestly deny that the world won't be a better place if we all strive to live of life of virtue, enjoying the powerful effect of these fruits?

Many are inspired, while others are confused by the life of saints and about why Catholics hold them in such high esteem. To this response, I will suggest that if we're being truly honest with ourselves, won't we all benefit from aspiring to be more like the saints? Saint John Paul II and Saint Teresa were perfect models of what it means to be fully alive. They conformed their will to God's will and lived in deep friendship with Jesus, who *is* the glory of God in the flesh. Saints are people among us who are striving to cooperate with God's grace and live in the fruits of the Holy Spirit. So how do we accomplish this in our ordinary lives? I believe that the more we choose to live in the fruits, the more they will actually grow in us. For example, we can daily

- *choose* to be loving to every person we encounter;
- *choose* to be joyful even in the most difficult times;
- *choose* to be peaceful in times of hardship;
- *choose* to be patient when our patience is tested;
- *choose* to be kind to those who are unkind;
- *choose* to be gentle even when we're tempted not to be;
- *choose* to be generous with our time, talents, and gifts;
- *choose* to be faithful to prayer and vocation in our lives;
- *choose* to live in self-control when temptation surrounds us.

By continuing to stimulate ourselves physically, mentally, and spiritually and by seeking a healthy lifestyle in all aspects of life, we will live a more abundant and fuller life. By striving to be our best and having the courage and authenticity to let others share in our lives, we become more fully alive as we are constantly awakened to God, to others, and to ourselves. Our heightened awareness and gratitude, filled with His abundance of every good grace, makes all things possible. We are truly happier and healthier people living our lives filled with greater meaning and purpose. And after all, isn't life too short to be anything but happy and healthy?

NATURAL REMEDIES

An ounce of prevention is worth a pound of cure.

—Benjamin Franklin

FOREWORD

The greatest medicine of all is to teach people how not to need it.

I BREATHE IN THAT crisp morning breeze as I drive toward my favorite coffee shop. Pulling up to the drive-through, I hear eight wonderful words: "Welcome to Starbucks. How may I help you?"

"Good morning. I'd like a skinny coffee Frappuccino, please." As I sip on that 180 calories of goodness, my taste buds explode not only from the glorious flavor but also from the volcanic eruption of sugar exploding in my body.

During my high school years, this was one of my favorite rituals as a sixteen-year-old—young, of vibrant health (at least I thought at that time), and living carefree. "What a great way to start my day," I would tell myself. This "skinny" Frappuccino I so often ordered was not only low in calories but was also delicious *and* healthy for me. Or so I thought.

Knowing what I know now about the multitude of unhealthy ingredients in that drink, I shudder at the thought of what I was filling my body with at such a young age. This was just one of the many daily choices I was ignorantly making that contributed to my slow but steady decline in health.

The day I turned twenty-one, my health very noticeably started to deteriorate. I often woke up with little to no energy, my beautiful young skin began constantly breaking out, and my mind was slow and sluggish, which I now knew to be considered brain fog. Other symptoms included my period being inconsistent and painful, often with terrible PMS symptoms, and being full of anxiety or completely lacking motivation in my daily life. My zeal for life had been robbed from me, and I truly had no idea why or what was happening to me. I knew that something was wrong, that something was off, but I did not know what.

I thank God for protecting me from filling my body with pills and artificial substances, which I so easily could have done. Could I have gone on birth control for my PMS symptoms and period inconsistencies? Absolutely. Could I have gone on antidepressants for my anxiety and lack of zeal for life? Sure. But my gut was telling me to choose another route. (Side note: I 100 percent believe in the importance of modern medicine. It has saved my life while delivering my second child, but it should only be used when absolutely no other options are available.)

And so with my increasing health issues, I began praying and researching—and praying more and researching more. I begged God to help me discover what was wrong with me. Whether it was divine intervention or a crazy coincidence, I had this vision of bread one day while I was praying. (Crazy, right?) Maybe I was just hungry. But I thought maybe God was telling me that my health decline had to do with bread. I have since discovered I have gluten intolerance. This was contributing to brain fog, lack of energy, and some of my other symptoms. Looking back now, I realize God had slowly opened my eyes to understand the significance of what I was putting in my body and its correlation to my health and everyday well-being.

During this time in my life, I began a detox process. I was constantly researching and trying to discover how to best care for my body naturally. I took tests to discover my body's particular food sensitivities, and I began pulling anything out of my diet that did not bring vitality and health to my body. The more I learned, the more I wanted to learn. I desperately tried to heal my body from the years of food from my high school cafeteria and fast-food restaurants and passionately tried to fill my body instead with life-giving foods. With each day and each week, I noticed my health coming back to life. My skin began to clear, my energy came back, I was able to focus, my brain fog lifted, my period became regular, and my overall mood and outlook on life was full of hope and joy again. It was a process of months and even years, but I felt that my life was given back to me.

Whether it is choosing organic meat over hormone-filled meat, using peppermint oil to clear a headache instead of Tylenol, or avoiding chemically filled cleaners in your home and using more natural ones, there are small ways *every day* that you can positively contribute to the longevity of your health. These small choices we make every day have a significant impact on our long-term health. I thank God that I was able to experience a decline in my health at a young age so that I could learn the importance of my everyday choices, still have the time to reverse any damage, and prepare myself for a much healthier future.

My prayer for you is that the "Natural Remedies" section of mom's book, *Life Is Too Short to Be Anything but Happy and Healthy*, will open your heart and mind to the importance of natural remedies and taking ownership of your health. You have the power within you to change so much of your health and your life in a positive way. Take ownership of that.

Haylee Lindenau
Bend, Oregon

INTRODUCTION

M Y PASSION FOR good health and natural living has always driven me to share what I have learned about natural remedies for health promotion and illness prevention. And although it is true that the development and mass production of chemically synthesized drugs has revolutionized health care in most parts of the world during the past one hundred years, many people still rely on natural and herbal medicines. The use of natural health remedies also increases when conventional medicine has been ineffective in the treatment of disease, such as in advanced cancer and infectious diseases. Today natural remedies are commonly used in the prevention and treatment of a variety of ailments, including inflammation and chronic and acute conditions, as well as in an effort to boost the immune system and quality of life. Natural remedies can be taken in many different ways and forms, including whole herbs, syrups, teas, essential oils, rubs, capsules, and tablets that contain a ground or powdered form of the raw herb or its dried extract.

Natural and herbal remedies use the plant's seeds, berries, roots, leaves, bark, and flowers. Likewise, not only is the type of environment in which the plant grows important but also the way it has been harvested and processed. The major areas of concern with the use of herbs and plants are quality, safety, and production. As with the consumption of raw fruits, plants, and vegetables, it is imperative that only 100 percent organic and pure forms be used. Whether it's an essential oil, herb, prescribed medicine, or over-the-counter medication, all should be treated with respect and caution. Our age, health history, medications taken, and body chemistry are all key factors in personal health care. Likewise, it is crucial that we research and educate ourselves before we take anything, not only in examining the various benefits but also in the safely of its dosage.

With so many natural remedies readily available today, the need for expensive prescription medication can decrease drastically. Without a doubt, there are times when only prescription medicine will do, but natural remedies offer a vital role in our preventive health care. So if by using natural herbs and spices to supplement my diet I can focus on my overall health protection and maintenance, I wholeheartedly say, "Why not?" If daily natural remedies will help keep the doctor away, then I completely agree with Hippocrates when he says, "Nature itself is the best physician." Below is a compilation of my favorite natural remedies for health, beauty, and home care. I include everything from my favorite household cleaners and disinfectants to my very own survival bag and homemade Perfect Balm.

Allergies

D ID YOU KNOW that skin allergies prompt about 5.7 million doctor visits annually? Such is true according to the American Academy of Allergy, Asthma, and Immunology. We all seem to have at least one food, material, or product that our body just doesn't agree with. For many, it's food allergies; for some, it's environmental. And for others, it's substance allergies. For me, it's the adhesive of a Band-Aid. If I dare put a regular Band-Aid on my skin, the reaction is ten times worse than the cut. I have found that when I remove the Band-Aid, the cut has healed, but the skin under the adhesive part of the strip is red and inflamed. With the use of a hydrocortisone cream, the rash generally heals within a few days. But eventually, I have succumbed to the fact that I need to use hydrocolloidal bandages, and nothing else will do.

I'd never forget Christmas tree shopping one year when the kids were young. Baby Haylee was in a carrier on my back, Jimbo was diligently helping look for that perfect tree, and Bobby was climbing the trees in the Christmas tree lot. Next thing I knew, Bobby was covered in hives. Apparently, he was very allergic to the Norfolk pines of eastern

Tennessee. A quick decision was made, and we were off to get some Benadryl in Bobby.

And then there was my best friend's reaction to glue—highly allergic. Thank goodness Dianna and I decided to try eyelash enhancers several weeks before Haylee and Mike's wedding and not the day before. Within a day of having them glued on, her eyes had swollen to the size of golf balls. Who would have thought that tiny drop of glue could cause such a fierce reaction? They are life lessons definitely worth sharing with others.

The most prevalent food allergies are milk, eggs, fish, shellfish, tree nuts, peanuts, wheat, and soybeans. The most common products used daily by many that can also cause skin allergies and irritation to others are chemicals, fragrances, nickel, adhesive, and fabrics. With environmental allergies, it's our surroundings that are causing the problem. The top environmental allergy is—yes, you've guessed it—pollen. Others include dust mites, pets and animals, and mold and mildew.

So whether you find yourself sniffling, sneezing, coughing, or itching, pay attention to those allergies. As with most allergies, the more intense and frequent the exposure to the irritant, the more likely our allergic reaction develops and heightens, many times eventually resulting in complete intolerance.

Apple Cider Vinegar

IS APPLE CIDER vinegar (ACV) really the cure-all people say it is? I think so. Apple cider vinegar can be used to cook, to clean, and most importantly to improve our health. Apple cider vinegar has a long history of home remedy benefits, many of which are now supported by science, but did you know that ACV actually has a long list of health benefits as well? Just to name a few, this list includes reducing cholesterol, lowering blood sugar levels, improving symptoms of diabetes, balancing the body's pH, providing enzymes, improving digestion, and aiding in weight loss. The fermentation process of apple cider vinegar is critical to producing the primary beneficial ingredient found in the vinegar—acetic acid. The 5 to 6 percent concentration of acetic acid does contribute to the sour, pungent taste, but it is also responsible for the numerous health benefits of ACV.

However, we have to keep in mind that not all apple cider vinegar is the same. The best ACV is raw and unfiltered that still contains "the mother." The mother contains the enzymes, minerals, and probiotics necessary for health benefits. While regular consumption of apple cider vinegar can have a lot of health benefits, it's always a good idea to start with a smaller dose to observe its effects on your body because everybody's different. As a sidebar, I also like to note that if you drink it straight and accidentally inhale it, you can chemically burn your lungs. It's always important to remember that just because something is natural does not mean it is safe to use it in excess.

What's the best time of day to take ACV? Some prefer taking apple cider vinegar first thing in the morning on an empty stomach. Some prefer it with meals or right before bed. I've read that it's kind of like the rinse cycle in the washer. Once the digestive and metabolizing systems have done their job throughout the night, the ACV can give the whole body a good final rinse without anything else getting in the way or stopping the process. So although any time is better than not at all, I choose to consume my ACV in the morning on an empty stomach. I chase 1 oz. with my favorite morning drink just before I take my vitamin and mineral supplements. Some like to add it to warm tea and sip on it, but I personally don't like to belabor it. I do it because it's good for me, not because I like the taste of it.

Apple cider vinegar is not only useful for health purposes but it's also useful for personal hygiene, cleaning, garden care, and much more. ACV is an inexpensive natural alternative to harsh commercial cleaners and can be used to clean and disinfect around the house, everything from floors to drains. Adding a cup of ACV to your next load of laundry will freshen both the laundry and the machine. It's a nontoxic and biodegradable alternative and has a much more pleasant smell than plain white vinegar.

Baking Soda

WHAT CAN WE use baking soda for? Just about everything. The uses of baking soda range from personal hygiene and beauty to deodorizing and cleaning the house. Commonly thought of as just the leavening ingredient that makes baked goods rise, baking soda also has numerous health benefits. It's one of those household staples that I'm never without, and it's less than a dollar a box. I have a box in the kitchen and every bathroom as well as the garage.

What is baking soda, and where does it come from? The baking soda chemical formula is $NaHCO_3$. For those like me who have forgotten everything they have ever learned about chemistry, its composition is that of sodium and bicarbonate ions. It is commercially mined here in America in both Colorado and California from a mineral known as nahcolite.

Let's first talk about the health benefits of sodium bicarbonate. It provides dietary bicarbonate, naturally made by our kidneys, that neutralizes stomach acid and relieves the many symptoms of acid reflux and other stomach-related health issues. Slowly drinking a teaspoon of baking soda in cold water helps neutralize acid and inflammation as well as improve the pH in the body. Recent research shows that baking soda may help improve cancer treatments as well as help slow the progression of chronic kidney disease (CKD). Because baking soda makes the environment less acidic, it can also help make the body and medicines work more effectively.

Believe it or not, human sweat is actually odorless. Sweat gains an odor after it is broken down by the bacteria in our armpits. Baking soda can help eliminate the smell of sweat by making the odor less acidic. Try rubbing your armpits with a little baking soda/water paste and see if the sweat odor doesn't disappear. A little baking soda paste can also be used to exfoliate skin, whiten teeth, and freshen breath. However, if we use too much baking soda, we can upset the pH balance of our skin, causing irritation. The general rule of thumb with any new health remedy is to start slow, introducing it to your body one to three times weekly before adding to your daily routine. One of my favorite uses for baking soda is in the bath. Try adding ½ cup to your next soak, along with your favorite bath salts and essential oils, and you're in for a soothing and relaxing treat.

Because I like to eat the skins of many of the fruits and vegetables I consume so as not to lose the important nutrients such as the fiber, vitamins, and minerals found in the skins, I started washing my fruits and vegetables—organic or not—in a baking soda wash just to be sure. Soaking in one teaspoon of baking soda and cold water for fifteen minutes provides great peace of mind that if there was a trace of anything undesirable, it's gone.

And as for household cleaning, it's the best multipurpose cleaner I've found. It not only whitens and disinfects but also freshens and deodorizes. But my favorite household tidbit is saving the scorched pot or pan. Twice this year, I walked away from boiling eggs and inadvertently scorched the bottom of my small saucepan. I tried several things, including soaking, scrubbing, and lemon juice, before I remembered the baking soda save. Just sprinkle a generous amount of baking soda over the bottom of the pan and add enough water to cover the burnt area. Bring to a boil, and the scorch is gone.

So in a nutshell, it's inexpensive, and it's readily available. Why not use baking soda for just about everything?

Blood Type

DO YOU KNOW your blood type? How does your blood type affect how your body processes food? Are there vitamins and supplements that work best in your body but not in mine? As with all health studies, there are opposing views about whether our blood type determines which foods work best with our internal chemistry. I certainly concur with a healthy diet of whole foods, plenty of leafy greens, lean proteins, and healthy fats and the avoidance of white sugar and grains; but if a certain blood type seems to require a little more or less of a particular food type for optimum levels of digestion and nutrition, then it's certainly worth giving some thoughtful consideration.

The studies go something like this. For those of us with type O blood, we are said to do best with a largely plant-based diet with lean meats, cutting out wheat and dairy. If we have type A blood, we do best with carbohydrates, cutting out meat altogether. And if we have Type B and type AB blood, we do best with a balanced omnivorous diet. I have type O blood, and I couldn't concur with this study more.

Primarily, the main diet issue for people to consider based on their blood type is the level of hydrochloric acid produced in the stomach. Hydrochloric acid is essential for properly digesting food, especially animal protein. Substantial scientific evidence demonstrates differences in hydrochloric acid levels based on our blood type, with type O blood having the highest levels and, likewise, increased risk of developing gastric ulcers. Blood work reveals vitamin and mineral deficiencies, as well as how well our kidneys and liver are functioning, so obtaining this information every few years helps us assess what our dietary needs are and if any adjustments are needed.

When I had this blood work done, it confirmed not only some of the foods that did and didn't work well with my system but also the ones I seemed to crave periodically. It was not a coincidence that, from a dietary perspective, I discovered at a very young age that my digestive system required higher levels of fiber to protect me from severe indigestion, cramping, and constipation. I instinctively chose a vegetable-rich diet, which concurred with these studies on my blood type, O.

Bug Spray

16 oz. distilled water
Citronella
Eucalyptus oil
Lavender oil
Neem oil
Peppermint oil
Tea tree oil

I KEEP TWO SPRAY bottles ready to use at all times. When spraying plants, pathways, or seating areas, I use tap water. When spraying people or pets, I use equal amounts of distilled water and witch hazel. Not only is a natural bug spray cost effective but it can also be used on all skin types and children without causing any type of skin irritant or rash.

Add two full droppers of essential oils to 16 oz. water to achieve desired scent. Other optional oils that can be added are clove, lemongrass, and rosemary. The more oils used, the stronger the spray will be.

I've discovered that with a 4 oz. bottle of essential oil, a full dropper is about twenty drops. Likewise, when I prepare a larger 32 oz. spray bottle, I use two full droppers of each of my desired oils.

Calcium Works Best with Magnesium and D$_3$

FOR YEARS, WE have been told to make sure we get enough calcium as it is good for our bones. And although calcium is one of the most important trace minerals involved in helping promote bone health and preventing and treating osteoporosis, research reveals that magnesium and vitamin D are also key nutrients for bone health. Magnesium helps keep calcium in the bones where it's needed and out of the soft tissues while Vitamin D helps facilitate the absorption of calcium. It's a combination of these three nutrients that optimizes bone health.

While calcium and magnesium are minerals that are both important for bone density, they have opposite effects on nerve, muscle, and clotting activity. Calcium stimulates activity, and magnesium actually relaxes or decreases activity. Because calcium works so closely with magnesium, it is important to have an appropriate ratio of both minerals for them to be effective. A good rule of thumb is a 2:1 ratio of calcium to magnesium. If we take a supplement that has 1,000 mg of calcium, then our magnesium supplement should be 500 mg.

In addition to providing structure to bones and body tissues, magnesium is actually needed for more than three hundred biochemical reactions in the body. It also assists in the release of energy from fat and carbohydrates consumed, helps with the stability and proper functioning of DNA production, and supports nerve impulses, muscle contractions, and normal heart rhythms. Although we only need small amounts of magnesium relative to other nutrients, the body loses magnesium every day from normal functions such as muscle movement, heartbeat, and hormone production. Likewise, it is recommended that we regularly replenish our stores from fresh foods or supplements to prevent a deficiency.

There are many reasons why deficiencies are so common today. A few factors at play are the depletion of nutritional value of soil, resulting in less minerals and vitamins in our crops; digestive disorders leading to improper absorption of magnesium and other minerals; and high usage of prescription medication and antibiotics damaging the digestive tract to the point that the nutrients cannot be absorbed and properly utilized from foods. It is estimated that 80 percent of all adults are deficient in this vital mineral. Although a magnesium deficiency can often be overlooked, it has been identified with muscle aches and spasms, poor digestion, constipation, high blood pressure, anxiety, insomnia, nausea, and vomiting.

While fresh, organic foods are always the best option, it is a good idea to think about taking a whole food supplement, considering all the important roles that calcium and magnesium play in the body regularly. Calcium-rich foods include milk, yogurt, cheese, enriched breads, fortified cereals, and dark leafy greens such as spinach, kale, turnips, and collard greens. Magnesium-rich foods include brown rice, dark green vegetables such as spinach, beans, nuts, seeds, and whole grains.

A supplement should be just as pure and natural as fresh food. Make sure no other additives or fillers have been included. Look for chelated forms of both nutrients because it is the easiest form for the body to absorb. Chelated forms of calcium are calcium citrate, calcium lactate, or calcium gluconate. The daily recommended amount of calcium is 1,000 mg to 1,500 mg. Chelated forms of magnesium are magnesium glycinate, gluconate, and citrate. The daily recommended amount of magnesium is 310 to 420 mg.

It would be remiss not to mention that vitamins D and K also play key roles in promoting bone health. Vitamin D plays a critical role in maintaining bone density when taken with calcium. Vitamin D also helps enhance calcium absorption in the body and with bone formation. In other words, without enough vitamin D, we aren't able to use all the calcium that we're taking in. The absolute best source of vitamin D is the sun. Just fifteen minutes of sun exposure a day will substantially boost our vitamin D production. Food sources that are high in vitamin D include cheese, egg yolk, fortified milk, fish liver oils, and salmon. The daily recommended amount of vitamin D is 400 to 800 IU for adults under the age of fifty and 800 to 1,000 IU for adults over the age of fifty.

Vitamin K helps promote strong bones by binding calcium and other trace minerals to the bone. Food sources that are high in vitamin K are broccoli, brussels sprouts, cauliflower, chickpeas, dairy products, kale, eggs, and nuts. The recommended dosage of vitamin K is 150 mcg a day.

With all the research available today, it's easy to think that we can diagnose and medicate ourselves better than anyone else. However, as with all supplements, it's always best to speak with a doctor before taking anything that might interact with other common medications we might be taking for high blood pressure, antibiotics, or diuretics. Equally important is the proper amount of the supplement. Just as a deficiency can cause health issues, an overabundance can flare up another whole set of health concerns. Because healthy, balanced levels of calcium, magnesium, and D_3 promote better sleep, I take these three mineral supplements at night.

Coconut Oil Pulling

OIL PULLING IS an age-old remedy that uses the natural substance of coconut oil to clean and detoxify our teeth and gums. In addition to pulling harmful bacteria out of the gums, oil pulling naturally whitens the teeth. Simply place a heaping teaspoon of coconut oil in the mouth and swish it around for about twenty minutes. Interestingly enough, timing is the key to oil pulling—not too much, not too little. Twenty minutes is just long enough to break through the plaque and bacteria but not long enough that the body starts reabsorbing the toxins and bacteria.

The swishing action is able to cut through plaque and remove toxins without disturbing the teeth or gums, improving overall oral health. Basically, the oil binds to the biofilm—otherwise known as plaque—on the teeth and reduces the amount of bacteria in the mouth. Remember, do not swallow the oil and be sure to spit all the oil out in a trash can as it now contains any and all toxins and bacteria that have been in the mouth. I like to rinse well with my homemade mouthwash and then brush as usual to make sure any remaining bacteria is removed.

So although *oil, pulling,* and *teeth* in the same sentence may arouse ill feelings, oil pulling is nothing more than using a high-quality organic oil such as coconut oil as a mouthwash to help thoroughly cleanse the mouth. Any carrier oil can be used for oil pulling so long as the oil used is food grade and edible. I personally prefer to use coconut oil for several reasons. Coconut oil is effective in attacking *Streptococcus mutans* bacteria, which is one of the bacteria prominent in the mouth and has been studied for its role in tooth decay and gum disease. Coconut oil is rich in medium-chain triglycerides (MCTs), which as recent studies show are a naturally occurring source of dietary fats that our bodies rapidly convert into ketones, which can be used as a fast energy source and likewise are less likely to be stored as fat.

Coconut oil can aid in better digestion, improved bone health, and superior metabolic function and even an enhanced immune system. It offers many benefits not just to us humans but also to our animal companions. Just a teaspoon a day can aid in making Fido's skin healthy by clearing up common skin problems such as itchiness, allergies, fungal infections, eczema, and contact dermatitis. It not only prevents dry skin, making his coat soft and silky, but it also disinfects cuts and promotes wound healing.

Because coconut oil is my oil of choice for just about everything from oil pulling to creamer in my coffee and it has dozens of uses, I have a jar in the kitchen and bathrooms. Again, not all coconut oils are the same. I choose to use expeller-pressed and refined oil from organic coconuts. If I'm going to use it, I'm only using the best.

Collagen Supplement

COLLAGEN IS THE most abundant protein in our body, making up about 30 percent of our whole-body protein content. It is one of the major building blocks that provide structure to our bones, skin, muscles, tendons, and ligaments. Serving as the connective tissue that holds all these parts together, the fibrous bands of collagen serve as the main support system of the dermis, the deepest layer of skin. In addition, collagen is in the stomach's connective tissue and helps support and strengthen the protective lining of our digestive tract. Needless to say, collagen is a major player in our total health and wellness.

As we age, our body produces significantly less collagen. In fact, after the age of thirty, we lose 1 percent of our collagen level every year thereafter. Likewise, it is never too soon to start protecting our collagen against future damage and begin storing up the skin's collagen layer. While there are plenty of choices to add a daily dose of collagen such as a high-protein diet found naturally in beef, chicken, fish, and egg whites, sometimes a supplement is the most effective and consistent source.

The right collagen supplement is a multisource collagen peptide that includes the five main types of collagen—Types I, II, III, V, and X. In total, there are over sixteen kinds of collagen found in our body, but these are the primary ones we need to continually supplement.

Type I: This type accounts for 90 percent of your body's collagen and is made of densely packed fibers. It provides structure to skin, bones, tendons, fibrous cartilage, connective tissues, and teeth.

Type II: This type is made of more loosely packed fibers and is found in elastic cartilage, which cushions our joints.

Type III: This type supports the structure of muscles, organs, and arteries.

Type IV: This type helps with filtration and is found in the layers of our skin.

Type V: This type of collagen is needed to make the surface of cells, as well as hair strands.

Type X: This type helps with the formation of new bones and articular cartilage. It's also been found to be helpful in the healing and repair of bone fractures and synovial joints.

The benefits of a multicollagen supplement include supporting joint health; revitalizing skin; promoting healthier hair, nails, teeth, and gums; balancing hormones; improving digestion; and supporting weight loss. Because our body repairs and regenerates while we sleep, one of the absolute best times to take extra collagen protein is right before bed. And because collagen doesn't put excess stress on our digestive system, it doesn't leave us with a heavy feeling that disturbs our rest. Collagen, along with calcium, magnesium, and vitamin D_3 are the supplements I take at night.

The abundance of collagen produced in our body is easy to overlook and take for granted. However, as we mature, we simply break it down faster than we can replace it. Injectable fillers composed of collagen have been introduced in the United States in the 1980s, but they are both temporary and expensive. Supplementing our body's production with a multisource collagen peptide daily after the age of thirty will help maintain a higher collagen level continually.

Cough and Congestion Relief

THERE ARE SEVERAL natural remedies specifically helpful for cough and congestion relief that have antibacterial, antispasmodic, antiviral, and expectorant properties. As with other natural remedies for health care, they offer a safe and effective way of getting rid of the cough, congestion, and other symptoms of respiratory conditions that come with the common cold. Some of my favorite remedies for relief of these symptoms include both internal and external treatments such as consuming lots of fresh fruits and vegetables containing vitamin C and using essential oils, which both cleanse and boost the immune system.

My all-time favorite is adding a fresh lemon slice to every glass of water, which is a miracle worker for improved overall health in and of itself. In addition, the most effective natural remedies beside lemons are honey, carrots, garlic, and elderberry syrup, as well as eucalyptus, lemon, oregano, peppermint, and tea tree essential oils used in a diffuser and chest rub. The essential oils not only address the cause of the symptom by killing bacteria, toxins, and viruses but they also work to relieve our cough and congestion by loosening mucus, relaxing the muscles of our respiratory system, and allowing more oxygen to get into our lungs.

My next all-time favorite is honey. It serves as a natural cough suppressant and helps soothe a sore throat. Just two teaspoons of honey throughout the day and thirty minutes before bedtime will make all the difference in the world. I like to use local raw honey. Studies show that because it is left in its completely natural state, local raw honey contains pollen, enzymes, antioxidants, and many other beneficial compounds obtained from the surrounding environment that help build an immunity to seasonal allergies as well.

Another natural cough suppressant is carrots. As we know, carrots are good for our eyes. In addition, carrots are also very effective for removing cough and phlegm from the lungs and in treating asthma, bronchitis, and other respiratory problems. Carrots can also strengthen the immune system and promote regular bowel movements. They are an excellent source of vitamin A and beta-carotene as well as abundant in vitamins B, C, and K and minerals such as calcium, potassium, magnesium, manganese, and phosphorus.

Not too long ago, I have discovered this recipe using carrots and honey as a natural cough suppressant. Being a bit of a health nut, I like to try the natural remedy first. Cut three to four carrots into slices and boil until they become soft. Save the water in an 8 oz. mason jar. Remove carrots from heat and mash with fork or in a blender. Add carrots and four teaspoons of honey to water in the jar. Shake well and keep in the refrigerator. Take three to four spoons throughout the day, and in a few days, the phlegm will be gone and the cough eliminated. It has worked for me.

Garlic has also been used over the years to treat a little bit of anything that ails you, but science-backed studies actually prove that garlic's health benefits include antiviral, antibacterial, and antifungal properties. In addition, it also contains anti-inflammatory and pain-relieving properties. And when eaten, garlic helps boost the immune system and fight infection. Because my congestion always seems to settle in my sinus cavity, causing my ears to pop and sometimes ring, I now use garlic drops to help relieve and hopefully prevent any infection that might have begun in the inner ear.

It was suggested that elderberry's reputation as a healer may have originated with Hippocrates, the father of medicine. He referred to elderberry as his "medicine chest" back in 400 BC. Elderberry was called a holy tree during the Middle Ages as it was believed to have the ability to preserve health and lengthen life.

Elderberry is the superberry of all berries and a real powerhouse for general well-being with its anti-inflammatory and antioxidant properties. It not only helps relieve the cough and congestion of common colds but also helps fight the flu and boost the immune system. I have discovered that elderberry, specifically known as *Sambucus nigra*, is now available in syrups, tablets, capsules, and even gummies. It's my new go-to for overall health, and I wouldn't go a day without it.

Last but certainly not least, just a few drops of lemon essential oil in a diffuser as well as a vapor rub will also help relieve cough and congestion. I like the smell and feel of lemon oil so much that I started adding it to my Perfect Balm and my bedroom diffuser daily. I rotate three to five drops of lemon oil with three to five drops of my other favorite diffuser scents of lavender and eucalyptus oils. Once or twice a week, I add tea tree oil for its added benefits. For additional relief and comfort, I add two drops of eucalyptus and lemons oils into half a teaspoon of the Perfect Balm and massage it on my neck and sinuses multiple times a day. This helps drain the lymphatic system while simultaneously loosening mucus, reducing cough intensity, and relaxing the muscles. Because these essential oils have antioxidant and anti-inflammatory properties, I have also found them to be extremely effective in treating the congestion I get with seasonal allergies. If the Benjamin Franklin axiom "An ounce of prevention is worth a pound of cure" is as true today as it has been when he's said it, I'm all in.

Decongesting Chest Rub

FOR ME, THE common cold and flu always seem to settle in my sinus and eventually produce a lingering dry cough. In addition to oral cough and congestion relief, I have discovered that using a chest rub accelerates my recovery tenfold. When it comes to drawing out phlegm and mucus lodged deep within the lungs, nothing works better than a decongesting chest rub.

My grandsons had a cough that just wouldn't go away this past winter. And naturally, it flared up while they were sleeping. When I rubbed their chest and back with this rub, they were half asleep by the time I finished and stopped coughing for at least eight hours.

For this rub, I include the incredibly potent decongestant and soothing essential oils that provide calm and instant relief. While lavender contains strong analgesic compounds that help with falling asleep at night, eucalyptus and peppermint oils offer a cooling and relieving sensation that helps clear congestion in the airways. I add a little tea tree oil for its antimicrobial properties, just in case there is any bacteria lingering around. I also suggest adding your favorite essential oil to the mixture—you know, the one that makes you crave using it. You can never use too much of it, and the more you use the rub, the quicker the cough and congestion diminish.

8 drops eucalyptus oil
8 drops peppermint oil
8 drops lavender oil
8 drops camphor oil
4 drops aloe vera oil
4 drops tea tree oil
1/4 cup shea butter
1/4 cup coconut oil
2–4 oz. glass jar

Melt the shea butter and coconut oil in a double boiler. Pour into a small mason jar, add essential oils, and shake well. Rub over chest and back every night until the cough and congestion clears. If preferred, the rub can be kept in the refrigerator to add a cooling sensation to cough and congestion relief.

Detoxing

WHETHER IT'S ONCE a week, month, or season, it's a good idea to cleanse and detox our body regularly. I've never been one for the extreme measures of drastic diets or fasting, such as the elimination of certain food groups or drinking liquid meals for any extended period. I truly believe we are meant to take care of our body as the temple God has created it to be. Likewise, I've always felt more comfortable with the overall goal of striving for a healthy lifestyle and eating sensibly. In the long run, I think a continuous and consistent diet will nourish and protect the body so much more efficiently and effectively.

I like to detox regularly by adding the most effective ingredients of lemons, cucumbers, ginger, parsley, cinnamon, and apple cider vinegar to my daily diet. For me, these ingredients are easily added to the liquids I consume daily. I chase 1 oz. of apple cider vinegar with my first glass of refreshing detox water every day. My water literally becomes a healthy energy tonic.

I love cucumbers and pickles, but lemons are my fave. They are one of the staples in the kitchen that I try to always have in stock. But when I do run out, I also have my lemon essential oil, and one drop is all it takes. Lemon has a purifying, cleansing, and protective effect on the body. It helps defend the body against harmful pathogens and promotes detoxification through the blood and liver. Lemons also stimulate lymphatic drainage, which helps the body cleanse itself of wastes and toxins. I never go a day without it.

Filled with vitamin K, B vitamins, copper, potassium, vitamin C, and manganese, cucumbers alone can help us avoid nutrient deficiencies in our diet. Cucumbers also contain unique polyphenols and other compounds that help reduce the risk of chronic diseases and other ailments. Ginger adds powerful anti-inflammatory and antioxidant effects; parsley is full of antioxidants, vitamins, and minerals; and cinnamon helps regulate blood sugar levels, high blood pressure, and high triglyceride and high cholesterol levels.

Over the years, I have heard many theories for calculating how much water to drink every day; however, the standard daily recommended amount is half our body weight—no more, no less. It is always important to support our bodies by drinking enough water but especially when we are under the weather. It just makes good sense to me when it's referred to as the rinse cycle for the human body, and so I will repeat the theory once more. Once our bodies have digested and metabolized our food during the night, apple cider vinegar and the detox water rinse the body of any lingering debris, allowing the body to begin the day with a fresh start. It's a simple, easy, cost-effective way to detox the body every day.

Refreshing Detox Water

1 lemon
1 cucumber
1 tsp. powdered ginger
1 tsp. powdered cinnamon
1 tsp. chopped parsley
32 oz. water

Favorite Essential Oils

I N THE PAST decade, more and more people have turned to natural remedies in their approach to health care in an effort to be free of the worries of unwanted side and long-term effects of pharmaceutical drugs. Essential oils offer a healthy alternative for inflammation and pain relief, boosting the immune system, preventing and maintaining certain illnesses, enhancing relaxation and sleep, and purifying the air around us, to name a few.

I have found an essential oil for just about everything that concerns or ails me, and I continue to be amazed at all the new uses I discover for them. Likewise, I have accumulated quite a collection. Always looking for the best price, I prefer to purchase 4 oz. bottles, making sure it is 100 percent pure, natural, and of therapeutic grade. In this order, my favorite essential oils are frankincense, lemon, peppermint, tea tree, chamomile, eucalyptus, lavender, myrrh, rosemary, and thyme. If I were recommending a starter set, it would have these in it.

Frankincense essential oil is known as the "king of oils" and for good reason. Its healing benefits include disease prevention and anti-inflammatory properties. One drop of frankincense under the tongue every day can go a long way in warding off all that is detrimental to our health. Other essential oils I use every day are the calming and cleansing therapeutic oils of lemon, lavender, and peppermint. As for tea tree oil, I always say, "A drop or two goes a long way." It not only helps soothe and relieve painful and irritated skin with its anti-inflammatory effects but it also has antibacterial, antimicrobial, antiseptic, and antiviral properties. Chamomile, rosemary, and thyme are the top contenders for hair and skin remedies, so I include them in all my beauty products.

Many times over, I have read about the damage that any and all inflammation can do to our body. What most of us don't realize, though, is that if we research a little deeper, we will see that the body cannot protect or heal itself as long as it is inflamed, thus the substantial importance of key anti-inflammatory properties in our daily health care routine. Similarly, part of having a more efficient immune system is the regulation of any inflammation in our body. The immune system is actually quite amazing, continuously interacting with every system of the body to prevent and fight disease. One of the primary mechanisms of the immune system is the influx of white blood cells or lymphocytes, the main defense method the body has. When inflammation occurs in an unhealthy body, the influx of these cells goes overboard and becomes problematic. By regulating inflammation, essential oils are a powerful tool not only for acute illness such as cancer but also for chronic and autoimmune disorders such as rheumatoid arthritis, ulcerative colitis, Crohn's disease, and bronchial asthma.

It will be remiss of me not to mention here the difference between essential and essence oils. Essential oils are a concentrated hydrophobic liquid containing volatile aroma compounds from plants and are highly effective at carrying the essence of the ingredient they are cultivated from. On the other hand, essence oils are a flavoring ingredient mainly used to give the flavoring or aroma of the substituted ingredient in a recipe.

Essential oils are extracted through the process of distillation. The raw plant, including any or all of the following parts—flowers, leaves, wood, bark, roots, seeds, or peel—of the original ingredient, is steam distilled. The steam, which is created as the water heats, passes through the plant material and vaporizes all the volatile compounds. The vapors then flow through a coil, where they condense back to liquid, which is collected, packaged, and sold. The most common essential oils are frankincense, lavender, peppermint, and eucalyptus and can be used in beauty products, perfumes, soaps, various household cleaning products, and aromatherapy.

Essence, on the other hand, is used primarily as a flavoring ingredient to give a recipe the flavor or aroma of the substituted ingredient. Natural essences are obtained by extracting the essential oils from the blossoms, fruit, roots, and other parts of the plant of spices, nuts, herbs, fruits, and some flowers. It can be either a highly concentrated form of pure extract or an imitation extract as the process to produce essence oils can be one of four methods of expression, absorption, maceration, or distillation. Concentrated essences are very strong extracts that can be twice to four times as strong as normal extracts. Commonly used essence oils are almond, cinnamon, clove, ginger, lemon, nutmeg, orange, peppermint, pistachio, rose, spearmint, vanilla, violet, and wintergreen.

When purchasing oils, always check the label on the bottle as it should specify if it's essential, pure, natural, and of therapeutic grade.

Ginger

I DON'T KNOW WHAT it is about ginger, but I just love it. Its distinctive spicy sweetness and invigorating kick make it a delightful addition to many food and drink recipes. That tablespoon of ginger that comes with most sushi dishes is not nearly enough for me. And don't even get me started on gingersnap cookies. They are always to be found in my grandparent's snack drawer and served with a cup of tea in the afternoon. This nana always has a stash in her cookie jar as well.

Ginger is a plant native to warmer parts of Asia—such as China, Japan, and India—but can now be found worldwide. Ginger can be used fresh, dried, or powdered or as an oil or juice and is the key ingredient of the stomach-settling ginger ale. Most commonly used as a spice, ginger is added as a flavoring agent but is also used as fragrance in soaps and cosmetics. A combination of ginger essential oil and spearmint or peppermint oil can be used in the diffuser to help with nausea, vertigo, or morning sickness. Besides being one of the most delicious and fragrant spices on the planet, it is also one of the healthiest. Likewise, ginger has a very long history of use in various forms of traditional and natural medicine.

Ginger is loaded with nutrients and bioactive compounds that have powerful benefits for our body and brain. The unique flavor and fragrance of ginger comes from its natural oils, the main one being gingerol. Gingerol is the main bioactive compound in ginger and has powerful anti-inflammatory and antioxidant effects. Research supports that ginger consumption is a significant relief for patients suffering not only from arthritis and muscular pains but also from diseases that are caused by cell inflammation such as diabetes, obesity, and Alzheimer's. Studies also show that ginger may help fight cancer cells and stimulate blood circulation in addition to stabilizing glucose levels in the blood and stopping acid reflux.

Household Cleaning Disinfectants

I LIKE TO STEER away from bleach and alcohol, so for everyday cleaning of kitchen and bathrooms, I use white vinegar and baking soda to clean and disinfect. As I've said before, baking soda is my go-to for just about everything. And when baking soda is added to white vinegar, I find I no longer need to purchase expensive and, might I add, toxic cleansers. White vinegar is also a safe and natural mold and mildew killer. A study by microbiologists at *Good Housekeeping* has discovered that white vinegar is 90.0 percent effective against mold and 99.9 percent effective against bacteria.

Although the smell of white vinegar will quickly dissipate, I like to add my favorite essential oils to the spray bottle to make it more pleasant. Some essential oils will actually boost the vinegar's mildew-killing power, such as grapefruit seed, lemon, and tea tree oil. These natural oils have antifungal properties of their own and help kill toxins and bacteria. Tea tree oil is the most effective essential oil I've come across. So when cleaning mildew off sidewalks, steps, and deck furniture, I add two teaspoons of baking soda and tea tree oil to a bucket of half vinegar/half water, and it works like a champ.

I fill a spray bottle for everyday use and make a paste when I'm deep cleaning. I use a thirty-two-ounce spray bottle that I fill with pure water and a little bit of white vinegar, to which I add three droppers full of lemon oil and tea tree oil. When I'm cleaning windowsills and doors, I add a little peppermint oil to ward off ants and spiders as well. These natural cleaning products are safe and effective and can be used on anything.

Insect Sting Relief

MIX TOGETHER FOUR parts baking soda to one part white vinegar to create a paste that can be rubbed on any and all insect bites for immediate relief of itching and irritation. Within minutes, the sting will go away. As it dries, it leaves a residue that feels like beach sand and can be wiped off with a wet washcloth.

While I was watering hanging baskets above my head late one summer afternoon, I stuck my finger in a wasp nest and was stung multiple times. I've never seen a finger swell so much and so fast in all my life. I immersed my whole finger in my jar of paste and let it sit there for almost an hour until the swelling and the throbbing finally subsided.

I keep a batch in a 4 oz. mason jar ready for use at all times. If the paste hardens, just add a little more vinegar and stir.

Lemons Simply Make Life Better

I CAN'T SAY ENOUGH about the value of lemons. Lemon is no longer considered just a garnish or a cooking ingredient and is commonly used for nonculinary purposes such as in home remedies. The most popular use of lemons is most likely to make lemonade by mixing the citrus fruit's juice with water. Nonetheless, it has always been used as a washing agent as well because of its ability to remove stains. However, what most of us probably didn't know is that lemons have also been used to help cure a multiple number of diseases and ailments for centuries.

Lemons are a good source of vitamins B_1, B_2, B_3, B_5, and C; calcium; magnesium; iron; minerals; and antioxidants. Likewise, lemons help boost health and well-being in several ways. The health benefits of lemons are attributed to its many nourishing elements that not only help improve digestion and encourage weight loss but also improve the quality of skin, hair, and teeth. Lemons can also help strengthen our immune system against the germs that cause common cold and flu, cleanse our stomach and digestive tract, and purify our blood. And the list goes on and on.

After exploring lemon facts, I have made lemons an integral part of my personal as well as home care. Once I have been aware of the many amazing uses of fresh lemons, I've had to ask myself if lemon essential oil could even be better than fresh lemons for certain purposes. Lemon essential oil is very high in limonene compared with fresh lemon, making it the more powerful antioxidant as well as cleansing agent. What's more, it has a longer shelf life and likewise won't need to be purchased as often. And so the answer is yes, lemon essential oil has its own laundry list of significant home and health-care benefits.

Lemon essential oil is best known for its ability to cleanse toxins from the body, fight bacteria and fungi, and stimulate lymphatic drainage. But it can also be used for everything from natural teeth whitener to mood booster and nausea reliever. It is also highly effective at rejuvenating energy. Its health benefits have been well documented in scientific studies, and it can be used in almost all our DIY beauty and cleansing products.

Another awesome use for lemon essential oil is removing stale smells. Ever go to use your cooler and open it up, only to find that it stinks? I have discovered that lemon essential oil is the perfect prevention for that. Simply place a paper towel in the bottom of the cooler, sprinkle a few drops of lemon essential oil on the paper towel, and close the cooler. Next time you use it, you will be pleasantly surprised by the fresh scent of lemon rather than the stale old smell from nonuse.

I pick up raw milk from a local farmer, and I use a couple of recycling bags from the grocery store to carry it. Unfortunately, I have noticed that the inside of the bags are starting to smell like spoiled milk. I have sprayed them clean with my tea tree oil and peppermint household cleaner spray, and all is well; however, the next time I have used them, the smell is back. So I now place a single sheet of paper towel at the bottom of each bag and regularly place several drops of lemon essential oil on it. Replacing the paper towel monthly keeps my recycling bags smelling fresh.

Most recently, I have put a paper towel with lemon essential oil drops inside my front-loading washing machine and kept it there until I used it again. Wow, what a pleasant surprise! Next come the dishwasher and refrigerator. From a cooler to an appliance to the car, everything will be that much fresher smelling. But don't forget, the lid or door must be tightly closed for maximum effect. Grab a bag of lemons and lemon essential oil at the market today and see if they don't help make life healthier, happier, and more beautiful.

Master Grocery List

MANY YEARS AGO, I have compiled a master grocery list on my computer; today it's on my phone so that all I have to do is print it out and highlight what I need from the store. I have also discovered that it is a really great way of sharing the brands that I desire when someone else is doing the shopping. I have added the reported top ten healthiest foods to the top of the list, to which I have included six more, as a reminder to stock them at all times.

Lemons, avocado, garlic, sweet potatoes, broccoli, spinach, lentils, salmon, walnuts, dark chocolate, cucumbers, blueberries, mushrooms, pumpkin seeds, and sunflower seeds.

GROCERIES

Fresh flowers
Chicken/salmon/fish
Meat/bacon/prosciutto
Fruit mix/vegetable mix

Kale-lettuce mix
Cucumbers/avocados
Lemons/limes/mint/cilantro
Apples/bananas/oranges
Berries/chickpeas
Tomatoes/green peppers

Red onions/scallions/ginger
Celery/carrots/red potatoes
Minced garlic/mushrooms/shallots
Sweet potatoes/cabbage
Asparagus/broccoli/cauliflower
Butternut squash
Sun-dried tomatoes/pesto
Beets/garlic/pickles
Ketchup/mayo/mustard
White beans/baked beans
Green/black olives
Campanelle/rigatoni pasta
Marinara sauce/tomato sauce/salsa
Coconut oil/olive oil
Sesame oil/honey
Chicken/beef broth
Baking soda
Lemon juice/soy sauce
White vinegar
Bragg apple cider vinegar
Red wine vinegar
Bragg vinaigrette dressing
Spices/Himalayan salt
Lipton onion soup mix
Cream of chicken/mushroom soup
Peanut butter
Sunflower seeds/walnuts
Sesame seed snack
Sandwich rounds
All-purpose flour
Raw sugar/brown sugar
Chili/taco seasoning mix
Stove-top stuffing mix
Truvia/sugar/stirrers
Coffee/vanilla rooibos green tea

Honey Nut Cheerios/granola
Guacamole/spinach dip
Blue Chips/pretzels/gingersnaps
Water/Gatorade/La Croix
Frappuccino/ginger ale
Sparkling water
Crescent rolls/focaccia
Milk/cream/cheese/eggs/butter
Cheddar/mozzarella/cream cheese
Fresh parmesan

HOUSEHOLD TOILETRIES

Lint rollers
Tea light/votive candles
Rejuvenate high-gloss restorer
Method wood cleaner
Cascade/dish sponge
Tide Pods/Downy booster
Pure liquid soap/Goo Gone
Paper towel/toilet paper
Napkins/Kleenex
Tupperware/oven liner
Tall kitchen bags
Large trash bags
Sandwich/snack/gallon bags
Easy-Off/Saran Wrap/Alum foil
Hydrogen peroxide
Distilled water/Epsom salt
Band-Aids/Aquaphor
Q-tips/hair clips/bobby pins
Glue/Scotch tape
Masking tape
Blink eye drops
Toothbrush/Plackers

Gillette Fusion blades
Box tape/blue tape
Envelopes/Doilies
Spotlights/chandelier lights
HP 63H Instant Ink black and color cartridges
Light bulbs/night light bulbs
AA/AAA/C/D/9V batteries
GE FXUVC house water filter
GE MWF refrigerator filter

SUPPLEMENTS

Almond/argan/avocado oil
Frankincense/myrrh oil
Lavender/lemon oil
Peppermint/tea tree oil
Ylang-ylang oil
Castile soap
Elderberry syrup
Magnesium
Multicollagen
Multivitamin
Probiotic and prebiotic
Turmeric

Multivitamin Supplement

I ALREADY KNOW WHAT your first thought is going to be because I've had the same one my whole life. Yes, I concur that the absolute best way of nourishing our bodies with the vitamins and minerals it needs is with good food. Food is medicine, and medicine is food. However, that being said, for many reasons, it seems next to impossible for most of us to get everything we need for our body from our food daily. So if we want to maintain our body at maximum efficiency and productivity, will we consider supplementing with whole food substitutes? For me, it's an absolute and resounding yes.

However, the key point to make here is that all multivitamins are not alike. It is the utter truth that many over-the-counter vitamin and mineral supplements are a complete waste of money. Don't even consider the synthetic ones. They are not only ineffective but can also be more damaging to our health than good. An organic whole food supplement is the only way to go. It is made from whole foods, not bits and pieces or divided parts. The whole food supplement is just that, made from real whole food, including powdered organic fruits, veggies, and herbs such as annatto, amla berry, holy basil, ginger, lemons, peppermint and many other real foods that help provide the natural nutrients that whole food offers. Why whole foods? Whole foods are plant foods that are processed and refined as little as possible before being consumed. Examples of whole foods include fruits, vegetables, legumes, tubers, and whole grains.

After researching a multivitamin supplement, I have chosen one that has everything I want it to have, including vitamin A, vitamin C, vitamin D, vitamin E, vitamin K, thiamine (vitamin B_1), riboflavin (vitamin B_2), niacin, vitamin B_6, folate, vitamin B_{12}, biotin, pantothenic acid, calcium, iron, iodine, magnesium, zinc, selenium, manganese, and chromium. Additionally, I like to add supplements of multicollagen, turmeric, prebiotic, and probiotic to my daily intake of vitamins and minerals.

Perfect Balm for Face and Body

ALTHOUGH I AM a strong believer that diet plays the largest role in how our skin looks and feels, skin care using pure and natural ingredients—including essential and carrier oils—will help create and maintain healthier skin. While essential oils such as frankincense encourage cell regeneration, carrier oils are absorbed safely and effectively, allowing our skin to retain a maximum amount of moisture, which is the key to a healthier, more radiant skin. Whether we are experiencing the early signs of aging, fine lines, irritation, or other skin imperfections, I truly believe pure and organic ingredients will help achieve the best results for our skin care.

I no longer purchase the expensive and many times chemical-filled health and beauty care products that inundate the market today. After years of research and trial and error, I created Perfect Balm. Below are the ingredients that I have discovered are the best choices for skin therapy. Perfect Balm is available online and in local health and wellness spas, but try making your own balm. Play around with it. I added turmeric and orange essential oil to my last personal batch. It's a little more yellow in color, but it smells like summer, and I love it. I like knowing exactly what's going on my skin as well as in my mouth.

Coconut oil
Shea butter
Aloe vera oil
Argan oil
Avocado oil
Castor oil
Cedarwood oil
Chamomile oil
Clary sage oil
Clove oil
Eucalyptus oil

Frankincense oil
Jojoba oil
Lavender oil
Lemongrass oil
Peppermint oil
Pomegranate seed oil
Rosehip oil
Rosemary oil
Tea tree oil
Ylang-ylang oil

Heat two cups of coconut oil and four cups of shea butter in a bowl over boiling water until they turn liquid. Pour into a one-quart mason jar. Add 1 oz. of carrier and essential oils. Shake until well blended and transfer to smaller glass jars.

As with anything new, I suggest starting small, perhaps using only on your face until accustomed to the feel, smell, and texture of the balm. I know I have mastered the ingredients when I have received a text from my world-traveling, missionary son, Jimbo, saying, "Mom, I am obsessed with this last batch of Perfect Balm."

Perfect Face Wash, Toner, and Mask

Face Wash

THE MOST ESSENTIAL ingredients that can be used to improve our complexion as well as leave skin soft and supple are lemon, lavender, and frankincense oils. I use a small spray bottle (8 oz.) filled almost to the top with spring water and add a dropperful of each essential oil. Over the years, I've tried cotton balls, facial sponges, and Coets, but my favorite is an organic wet wipe. By the time I've sprayed, wiped, and folded (three) times, I'm done. Three times a week, I add baking soda to my wipe for extra stimulation and exfoliation.

Face Toner

2 oz. pure aloe vera gel
2 oz. apple cider vinegar
2 oz. witch hazel
2 oz. water
Dropperful of chamomile essential oil
Dropperful of lavender essential oil

In an 8 oz. spray bottle, combine aloe vera gel, apple cider vinegar, and witch hazel with chamomile and lavender essential oils. Spray on face and neck, allowing to air-dry so that the anti-inflammatory and skin-enhancing properties soak in. Follow with Perfect Balm every morning and night.

Face Mask

2 teaspoons raw honey
2 teaspoons juiced lemon
½ teaspoon turmeric

Combine ingredients and spread over entire face, neck, and décolletage. Leave mixture on for twenty minutes and then rinse off. As a face mask, lemon and turmeric work to lighten the skin while honey eases any irritation or dryness, evening out your entire skin tone. It can also be applied as a spot treatment for affected areas such as age spots, sunspots, or acne scars. Remember, both lemon and turmeric can stain fabric, so use a rag towel over your pillow if you decide to take a nap.

Perfect Hair Wash, Conditioner, and Mask

Wash

AS THE SEARCH for alcohol-free organic hair products has begun, I have discovered that there just aren't that many to choose from, and the ones I have found are highly expensive. As with so many health and beauty care products, the best choice is in keeping it simple. I have found that the perfect hair wash for me is a mixture of baking soda and argan, peppermint, and tea tree oils. After wetting my hair, I prepare a paste of two tablespoons of baking soda with two drops of each essential oil in the palm of my hand and massage away. I rinse well and condition daily with leave-in conditioning spray or mask—no chemicals, no additives, and no alcohol to strip away the natural sheen of my hair. The hardest thing to get used to is the fact it's a paste and that there are no suds.

Leave-in Conditioner

I've tried many curling/styling hair products over the years but never discovered the one that is perfect for me. Curly hair requires the perfect amount of attention, not too much and not too little. Too much leaves it crispy, and too little leaves it flyaway. So after researching which essential oils are the best for hair, skin, and nails, I have compiled the following list: cedarwood, chamomile, frankincense, lavender, peppermint, rosemary, tea tree, and ylang-ylang.

Mix ten to twelve drops of each essence oil in a 20 oz. spray bottle of water for a moisture-rich, conditioning leave-in spray that never weighs the hair down. Whether leaving my hair natural and curly or blowing it dry, I use it every day. It can be reapplied as often as needed and never creates a buildup.

Mask

Once or twice a week, I give myself a castor oil hair mask and scalp massage. Castor oil is an antifungal and anti-inflammatory oil. It has the added benefit of increasing blood flow to the scalp, which can also increase hair growth. It is a wonderful moisturizer and nutrient-rich hair supplement and helps fuse together and moisturize split ends as well.

Apply a liberal amount of castor oil to palms. Starting at the scalp, work oil into all the hair, moving the fingertips in circles. I like to leave the oil in my hair for fifteen to thirty minutes in the morning while I catch up on e-mails. I then shampoo and condition my hair as usual. Since I have begun using all-natural and pure ingredients for my hair wash and conditioning, my hair has never looked or felt healthier.

Perfect Toothpaste and Mouthwash

Toothpaste

DENTAL CARE IS no exception to the rule when it comes to finding a natural, fluoride-free toothpaste that doesn't have extra ingredients or cost a fortune. As a result, it's back to the basics for me. Coconut oil, baking soda, and lemon essential oil is the best natural solution to improving overall oral and dental health as well as preventing oral disease. Place a dash, sprinkling, and dot of all three on a toothbrush and brush teeth for two to three minutes before rinsing.

Many years ago, I have begun spraying the toothbrush with hydrogen peroxide before and after each use to help keep germs at bay. As an added bonus, hydrogen peroxide also helps whiten teeth.

Mouthwash

The seven essential oils that make the list for the natural promotion of healthy teeth and gums are clove, orange, peppermint, cinnamon, lavender, myrrh, and spearmint. Clove, orange, and cinnamon are at the top of the list as the most effective in fighting against tooth decay and gingivitis and specifically aid with sensitive teeth, canker sores, and teeth whitening. Peppermint and spearmint help with freshening the breath.

While I have to admit that I used store-bought mouthwash for many years to help kill germs and freshen breath, there was something about it that just seemed too strong for me. An organic mouthwash is safe and effective and can also be used by children. I pour water and twenty drops of each essential oil into a 12 oz. plastic bottle with a flip top for spill-proof pouring. Individual bottles can be made for each family member.

Prebiotics and Probiotics

MANY ASK, "DO we need to eat both prebiotic and probiotic foods?" And the answer is a resounding yes. We need to eat plenty of both. They help promote the ideal balance between good and bad gut bacteria and keep our gut bacteria balanced, which is important for many aspects of our health. They are nutrition boosters that help enhance our immunity and overall health, especially GI health.

Prebiotics and probiotics support the body in building and maintaining a healthy colony of gut bacteria, which in turn supports and aids the digestion of foods. Prebiotics serve as fuel for probiotics;

hence, they are both needed. They help the good bacteria in our body thrive, resulting in its growth and multiplication. Prebiotics are present in fiber-rich foods such as artichoke, asparagus, banana, unrefined barley and oats, garlic, green beans, honey, leeks, onion, raisin, soybean, tomato, sprouted wheat products, and whole grains.

While prebiotics serve as the fuel, similarly, probiotics work as the engine. Probiotics, which are tiny living microorganisms, including bacteria and yeast, contain acid-resistant strains that support optimal digestive health and peak immune function. Probiotics are present in fermented foods such as dairy or soy yogurt with live cultures, kefir, sauerkraut, miso, unrefined whole grain breads, brined olives, and salted gherkins.

Surprisingly, apple cider vinegar is not a probiotic, according to research done by the U.S. Department of Agriculture's Agricultural Research Service, but rather a natural source of a prebiotic carbohydrate; and likewise, it is helpful in fueling probiotics. The key ingredient in raw, unfiltered apple cider vinegar is the fermented apples, which contain pectin. The pectin in the apple cider vinegar binds to waste products in the system such as cholesterol, harmful bacteria, and even toxins and pathogens and then carries the waste from our body by way of elimination, leaving the probiotics in our system to grow and continue to protect our gut. The result of this symbiotic relationship between prebiotics and probiotics is a total powerhouse for our body's digestive system.

Prebiotics and probiotics are found in everyday foods and can easily be added to our daily intake of good foods. For me, it's as simple as consuming two ounces of apple cider vinegar and a yogurt a day. But it never hurts to mix things up by regularly rotating the above-mentioned foods into our diet. They are also available in dietary supplements for those days when we just can't seem to get it all in.

As always, keep in mind that there are many, many kinds of supplements available today. When choosing a probiotic supplement, select one that guarantees at least a minimum number of spores at the time of opening and not at the time of manufacture (at least 1 billion). Some probiotics have been freeze dried, and some require refrigeration.

Studies show that health benefits are attained with dosages of 1 billion to 100 billion live organisms or colony-forming units (CFU) per day. I have found an organic probiotic blend that contains six strains of probiotics as well as a prebiotic in an organic vegan capsule for a little over $30 per month. Any organic supplement that only costs me a dollar a serving is worth having in stock for those days when I know I need to boost to my dietary intake.

Proper pH Balance

IF SOMEONE ASKED me a few years ago when the last time was that I thought about the acid/alkaline balance of my blood, my answer might just have been never. The only thing I've ever paid attention to has been my blood type. But a little bit of research reveals that proper pH levels are a crucial aspect to overall health. Health studies confirm that a balanced pH helps protect us from the inside out. The importance of reducing acidity and increasing alkalinity is, in fact, of great importance because disease and disorder cannot take root when the body pH is in balance. The pH balance refers to the balance of acid and alkaline in all fluids and cells throughout the body. The body needs a balance in the blood pH levels at a slightly alkaline level of 7.365 to stay healthy.

Because our diet plays a vital role in maintaining proper pH levels in the body, the most effective way to support a balanced pH is to eat nutrient-dense, alkalizing plant foods and to limit our intake of processed foods, milk and dairy, alcohol, caffeine, and grains. Consuming a more alkaline diet helps prevent tissues and organs from becoming damaged, unhealthy microbes and organisms from thriving, vitamins and minerals from being depleted, and the immune system from being compromised.

The toxic and acid-forming foods like processed sugars, refined grains, and genetically modified organisms that are found in a typical unhealthy diet lead to a damaging acidic pH level. Over time, an imbalanced pH can interrupt cellular activities and functions. When the body stays in an acidic state, it can lead to many serious health problems such as cancer, cardiovascular disease, diabetes, osteoporosis, and heartburn. Bad bacteria, viruses, candida overgrowth, and parasites all thrive in acidic environments, whereas an alkaline environment neutralizes bacteria and other pathogens. For that reason, maintaining our pH balance is one of the most important tools for optimizing our health.

Nobel Prize winner Dr. Otto H. Warburg has discovered that low oxygen is a characteristic of cancer cells. Oxygen deficiency results in an acidic state in the body. Dr. Warburg has also found that cancer cells do not breathe oxygen and cannot survive in the presence of high levels of oxygen as when the body is in an alkaline state. In his own words, "Cancer, above all other diseases, has countless secondary causes. But even for cancer, there is only one prime cause. Summarized in a few words, the prime cause of cancer is the replacement of the respiration of oxygen in normal body cells by a fermentation of sugar."

For those days when we've consumed everything acidic—coffee, milk, processed foods, ice cream, or alcohol—a quick and easy home remedy for neutralizing the acidity in our body goes back to three of my favorite staples: baking soda, fresh lemon juice, and organic apple cider vinegar.

½ tsp. baking soda
2 tbsp. fresh lemon juice
2 tbsp. organic apple cider vinegar

Pour the lemon juice and apple cider vinegar into an 8 oz. glass, add the baking soda until the fizz stops, and then fill the glass with water. This mixture will help neutralize the pH level, creating a more alkaline environment in our body, and it also helps with any stomach acid we might be feeling.

Nana's Survival Bag

Apple cider vinegar
Baking soda
Coconut oil
Collagen
Magnesium
Multivitamin
Perfect Balm
Peppermint essential oil
Pre- and probiotics
Tea tree essential oil
Turmeric
White vinegar

L IKE SO MANY before me, I decided that the best way for me to move forward in this second season of life was to commit to a simpler lifestyle. I began the process of cleaning and decluttering. Top to bottom, attic to basement, I can honestly tell you that I had gone through everything.

In many drawers and cabinets, I found products that were never opened, some that were half empty, and a few that had just one last squeeze left. What I came to realize was that so many products were what I would today consider toxic. As I removed these from my home, I discovered I didn't want or need to replace any of them. Suddenly, I realized I didn't need them now or ever again. And I also no longer needed to try the newest and the most advertised products anymore because I already used what I knew would be the healthiest, best choice for me.

When asked what a "survival bag" will look like—the items I just couldn't do without—I have come up with the above list of twelve cosmetics, toiletries, and cleaners I make sure I never run out of. For me, that means one open container and one in the cabinet. Refreshingly, I have several empty drawers and cabinets today, especially in guest rooms.

Turmeric

TURMERIC IS JUSTIFIABLY called the golden spice. And rightly so as it just may well be the most powerful herb of all the superfoods. Tens of thousands of articles have been published supporting turmeric's healing benefits of fighting and potentially reversing disease. Curcumin, which grows in Southeast Asian countries, is the active ingredient in turmeric and has a long history of being used as the main spice in any Indian curry dish. The distinctive yellow color and fragrance are the result of the fact that it is a member of the ginger family.

Turmeric curcumin health benefits include reducing pain and inflammation, regulating cholesterol, helping reduce the risk of blood clotting, and boosting skin health. There are many studies published that explore additional benefits of lowering glucose levels, reducing the growth of fat cells, aiding in digestion, and helping the liver efficiently detoxify the body naturally. A number of laboratory studies have shown that curcumin also has anticancer effects as well and that it not only seems to be able to kill cancer cells but also prevents more from growing.

The power health benefits of turmeric curcumin can be included in our daily health diet in recipes, essential oils, and supplements. Turmeric powder can be added to just about any recipe or dish before or after cooking. And by adding turmeric tea rather than that second cup of coffee to our daily health regime, we can help promote our health and wellness.

Turmeric is also available as an essential oil and in supplement form. As with most essential oils, you can use a drop in a smoothie or drink; however, I prefer to use oils in my daily balm and diffuser. Organic supplements are also available for daily consumption. The best turmeric supplements include black pepper for maximum absorbability.

What turmeric does for the body is nothing less than amazing, but as with any herb, turmeric might be an allergen to some, especially with skin exposure. Always err on the side of caution with all family members and use a small initial dosage, whether using turmeric powder, essential oils, or supplements. Whether it's reducing inflammation, aiding digestion, or simply improving our overall health, I suggest adding turmeric to our daily diet. Turmeric is in my survival bag, and I won't go a day without it.

Vitamin and Mineral Deficiencies

DID YOU KNOW that six of the most common health and beauty complaints are all due to vitamin and mineral deficiencies? I'm sure it will come as no surprise when I tell you that these symptoms that so many complain of, in this order, are headaches, low energy, stomach issues, acne and other skin irritations, hair loss, and brittle nails. These ailments affecting teens and young adults are also common among age-related health problems of older generations and are many times nothing more than symptoms of a common vitamin or mineral deficiency.

Our body needs vitamins and minerals for healthy development and daily functioning. Unfortunately, we are often unaware of these vitamin or mineral deficiencies until certain health conditions appear or already exist. Nevertheless, most of these deficiencies can be corrected quickly, easily, and inexpensively, making many of our health problems not only disappear but also eliminate further complications. As with every health issue or concern, "an ounce of prevention is worth a pound of cure" and vastly improves our total well-being.

One of the most common vitamin deficiencies is vitamin D. Vitamin D deficiency symptoms include general aches and pains, low energy, mood fluctuations, weak immunity, heart problems, vision loss, cognitive problems, and fragile bones, to name a few. Vitamin D is different from other nutrients in that it's a fat-soluble vitamin that isn't found in very many foods, all the more reason that it is imperative that our body be able to naturally produce it. Adequate vitamin D is necessary for its important role in regulating body levels of calcium and phosphorus and in mineralization of the bone. It is also essential for absorbing calcium, building and maintaining strong bones, and fighting infections.

Shockingly, it is reported that 75 percent of adults in the United States have low vitamin D levels. Vitamin D deficiency has reached epidemic proportions for one simple reason: we don't get enough sun exposure. There is a reason vitamin D is known as the sunshine vitamin. The majority of us now spend most time indoors rather than outdoors, and the human body can only produce vitamin D in response to the ultraviolet rays of the sun. When these ultraviolet rays touch our skin, it triggers our body to produce its own vitamin D. For this reason, moderate sun exposure is actually good for us. Sunscreens not only block 100 percent of vitamin D production but many also contain toxic chemicals that do more harm than good. There truly is substantial evidence in the claim that our health and wellness peaks during the summer months, when our body has an abundance of vitamins C and D.

That being said, there are only two ways to get the proper amount of vitamin D we need for optimum health benefits: spending several hours a day in direct sun exposure and consuming vitamin D. Because most of us don't have the luxury of being in the sun several hours a day, we need to supplement this nutrient. As with all supplements, fake Vitamin D is no good. D_2 is a synthetic version of vitamin D and has been proved by hundreds of studies to be poorly absorbed and less effective. The best supplement option is vitamin D_3, which is used in most whole-food dietary supplements. It is more absorbable and provides the most efficient benefits. According to the director of the nonprofit Vitamin D Council Dr. John Cannell, we should take supplements with 5,000 IU of vitamin D_3 daily to avoid deficiency and achieve optimum health benefits. This amount is eight times more than the government-set recommended daily allowance (RDA) of 600 IU.

It is equally important to note here that vitamin D doesn't work all by itself, and likewise, it's important to make sure we're getting adequate amounts of the other nutrients that team up with vitamin D to ensure optimal absorption and utilization within our body. Cofactors of vitamin D in building adequate amounts of vitamins and minerals in our bloodstream are iron, magnesium, zinc, omega-3 fatty acids, boron, vitamin K, vitamin B_7 (biotin), and vitamin C.

Iron is the mineral vital to the proper functioning of hemoglobin (red blood cells), a protein necessary to transport oxygen in the blood. It is also essential for the correct development and function of cells as well as the production of some hormones and tissues. Iron is one of the minerals that is crucial for the entire body, particularly for the hair. Initially, iron deficiency will lead to symptoms of fatigue, weakness, dizziness, headaches, and chest pains, among many others. Iron deficiency can also lead to hair loss as one of its key roles is to supply hair follicles with oxygen and important nutrients. Mild or moderate deficiencies in iron may not even be noticeable; however, a significant lack of iron will ultimately lead to anemia, when the body does not have enough hemoglobin in the blood.

Magnesium is a mineral involved in every stage of vitamin D metabolism and is critical to the proper utilization of vitamin D. Magnesium is also crucial to the proper functioning of the nervous system. Moreover, it prevents headaches, restlessness, and muscle cramps in its role of relaxing tense muscles. Magnesium can be consumed in green leafy veggies, such as kale or collard greens. Another great way to increase magnesium levels is to soak in an Epsom salt bath. Epsom salts are abundant in magnesium, and the skin absorbs it very quickly. So next time you know you will be sitting at the computer for more than a minute, soak your feet why you're at it. You'll be glad you did.

Zinc is another mineral needed to receive and absorb vitamin D. In the absence of an adequate amount of zinc, vitamin D will not be properly absorbed. Zinc not only colors and brightens our complexion but also is in charge of the control of oil production in the skin. Likewise, lack of zinc in the body can lead to the appearance of acne. A simple thirty milligrams of daily zinc can prevent the formation of acne, and this amount can be satisfied by consuming a quarter cup of raw pumpkin seeds. Zinc also accelerates the healing process by helping alleviate inflammation and regenerating skin cells. Those little white bumps so many experience on the upper back of arms are nothing more than a lack of essential omega-3 fatty acids. These essential fatty acids will actually inhibit the appearance of bumps because of their strong anti-inflammatory qualities. Omega-3 fatty acids are found in walnuts, chia seeds, flaxseeds, soybeans, and kidney beans.

Boron is a mineral that helps our body metabolize other key vitamins and minerals such as calcium, magnesium, and phosphorus. It plays a key role in bone health and also affects estrogen and testosterone levels. Boron is necessary for the rapid action of vitamin D on the cellular wall and, when deficient, can actually cause vitamin D levels to reduce further. Boron is found naturally in leafy green vegetables such as kale and spinach but can also be found in coffee, milk, apples, and dried beans.

Vitamin K is actually a compound vitamin, mostly of K_1 and K_2, and plays a key role in helping the blood clot, preventing excessive bleeding. It also works with vitamin D to make sure that calcium is stored in the bones and not on the walls of blood vessels, ensuring strong bones. Unlike other vitamins, vitamin K is not used as a dietary supplement, so it is imperative that we consume adequate amounts naturally. Vitamin K_1 can also be found in leafy green vegetables while K_2 can be found in meats, cheeses, and eggs.

Biotin, known as B_7, is a water-soluble B vitamin that helps our body convert food into energy. It helps us grow healthier and stronger hair and nails and improves the health of our skin. Although its deficiencies are not common, many people are biotin deficient, experiencing damaged and brittle hair and nails and even hair loss.

My cure-all is vitamin C, the one vitamin we can never consume too much of. As with many other vitamins and minerals, it actually enhances the absorption of other nutrients from plant foods as well as from supplements. In addition, vitamins C and D work together to support the body's immune system synergistically and to boost overall antioxidant levels.

Water

KEEPING HYDRATED IS crucial for our general health and well-being. The body is made up of about 60 percent water, and every single cell and organ of the body requires sufficient water to function properly. Some of the powerful health benefits of water include regulating our internal body temperature, lubricating our joints, and helping form saliva and mucus. Also, the water in our bloodstream metabolizes and transports the carbohydrates and proteins we consume in our food. In addition, the water in our system acts as a shock absorber for our brain, spinal cord, and fetus. And last but not least, water boosts skin health and beauty, improves energy levels, and boosts our physical performance. So as you can see, much of the water in our system is lost during everyday bodily functioning. Sweating, urinating, and even respiration all deplete the body's water supply; and therefore, it is imperative that we replace it regularly.

Studies show that the amount of water needed daily by each person may vary depending on how active we are, how much we sweat, and so forth. However, the general rule of thumb is that we should consume half our body weight in water every day. Generally speaking, around 80 percent of this should come from drinks, including water, and the rest from food. Add a slice of lemon to our water, and we've got the most inexpensive and refreshing drink available for aiding in digestion, helping maintain our weight, consuming vitamin C, and keeping our skin glowing.

Some of the water our body requires can be obtained by eating foods with a high water content, such as fruits, vegetables, and soups, but most comes from drinking water and other beverages. Drinking pure, clean water is, without a doubt, the best way of getting fluid for the body. Milk and juices are also good sources of fluid, but beverages containing alcohol and caffeine are not ideal because they actually dehydrate our system.

In discussing health-conscious choices for simple ways to reap the health benefits of water consumption, we can't forget about adding water to the largest organ of the body—our skin. Soaking in a bath, swimming, even wading in water will open the floodgates to restoring adequate amounts of water in our system. Body misting is another way to give our body a refreshing boost of water as well as essential oils. It will hydrate and rejuvenate our body at any time. I keep a few spray bottles around the house enhanced with my favorite essential oils for skin and hair as reminders to give myself a spritz. And speaking of essential oils, adding a diffuser to the family room, workroom, and bedroom will add water back into the air we are breathing.

And finally, let's not overlook all the benefits of soaking our feet. Immersing our feet in a pan of warm water not only helps us relax but also soothes our muscles, relieves aches and pains, and hydrates our skin. I have to admit that when I've sat down to edit this article, the first thing I have done is replenish my water bottle and pour a foot soak. Anytime, anywhere, a foot soak rocks.

Because our body is made up of so much water, it makes sense that we should strive to constantly replenish, cleanse, and feed our system with water. Staying hydrated by consuming plenty of water in any or all of the ways mentioned above is one of the easiest and healthiest daily habits we can adopt.

HEALTHY RECIPES

The doctor of the future will no longer treat the human frame with drugs, but rather will cure and prevent disease with nutrition.

—Thomas Edison

FOREWORD

ON A MILD evening in March, I walked into a stranger's home in Nashville for a house concert and walked out a few hours later, having made a sweet new friend, Deanna Mitchell. From the moment I met Deanna in her son's kitchen, I felt at home in her presence. With her bright smile and warm demeanor, Deanna extended a kind Southern welcome that endeared her to me right away.

But when our conversation turned to the world of food, nutrition, and health, I knew I had truly met a kindred spirit. As our conversation flowed easily from topic to topic, we discovered that we shared a love not only for the culinary arts but also for the way a homemade meal brought people together. Deanna's passion for food and wellness revealed her heart for hospitality.

I was honored when Deanna asked me to write the foreword for this section of her book, in part because I deeply love wholesome food and have found great delight in reading through each of her recipes but more so because I am incredibly grateful to link arms with such a creatively gifted woman as she shares her words, insights, and recipes with the world. Having developed recipes professionally for many years myself, I know firsthand the amount of effort that goes into constructing a solid recipe from start to finish. I admire Deanna greatly for her courage and commitment in crafting this collection.

On the pages that follow, you'll find Deanna's most loved and requested recipes. As you prepare them in your own kitchen and make memories of your own with this book in hand, I hope both your body and your soul are gifted with nourishment along the way.

In closing, I'm reminded of one of my favorite quotes from author Anthony Doerr. Upon reflecting on the culinary delights he has savored in Italy, he writes this gorgeous line in his book, *Four Seasons in Rome*:

"What we eat is a poem." Call me a romantic, but I sure do love that line. Wherever they take you, may your adventures in the kitchen invite you into the poetry, the joy, and the beauty of good food prepared with great love.

Hallie Klecker
Madison, Wisconsin

INTRODUCTION

WE ARE TRULY blessed with all the healthy food choices we have today. Most of us have an international cuisine selection within a five- to ten-mile radius of our work or home. And what with all the natural food stores that have opened up, we can purchase local, organic, and chemical-free ingredients for the times we chose to cook at home. I love doing both. Going out to dinner is a great treat, especially after a long day, but cooking at home for family and friends is possibly one of the best gifts of love and self we can give. I also have to admit here that I have become a bit of a food snob but in the best possible way. My goal is to prepare and consume the healthiest of food choices. And guess what? They are usually the most delicious choices as well.

So what exactly am I looking for with food choices? I am selecting ingredients that not only provide optimum nutrition and antioxidants to help fight illness and disease but also don't result in any type of reaction or inflammation. Research has proved that healthy foods are beneficial at a microlevel and provide protection against degenerative conditions that exist in the aging process. Fortunately, these same healthy food choices that fight inflammation are appetizing as well as easily accessible today.

Not too long ago, I have researched the top ten healthiest foods on the food chain, and I now keep them at the top of my grocery list. Here's what I have come up with: lemons, avocado, garlic, sweet potatoes, broccoli, spinach, lentils, salmon, walnuts, and dark chocolate. To this list, I have added kale-lettuce mix, chicken, cucumbers, mushrooms, blueberries, pumpkin seeds, and sunflower seeds. And there you have it. These are my everyday staples, and I try to make sure they are stocked in the kitchen at all times.

In an effort to create and maintain a healthy diet, I choose fresh, organic ingredients. If they are not available, I make sure to rinse fresh fruits and vegetables in a light vinegar or baking soda wash. I use fresh herbs and seasonings because they are always the tastiest and highest in value, but I do keep a few dried and powdered ones for backup. My favorite salts are Himalayan pink salt and sea salt. My favorite oils are coconut, olive, sesame, sunflower, and safflower oils. I have no problem using frozen vegetables; however, just as with herbs, fresh is always my preferred choice. When purchasing frozen fruits or vegetables, I make sure nothing else has been added. As for meat, fish, and poultry, you've guessed it—fresh, local, and organic choices are the best.

Using only the best ingredients available and the following collection of all-time favorite recipes, it is my hope that they will trigger your taste buds as well as a lifetime of loving memories. In collecting and organizing my favorite recipes from old note cards, notebook paper, and yes, even newspaper clippings that my grandmother, mother, or I had written on, I've realized that, many times, parts of a recipe are in my head and not on paper. Hence, I have attempted to clarify the ingredients as well as the directions and hope that they are clear and easy to follow. Blessings, peace, and bon appétit!

Cheesy Broccoli Bacon Dip

8 oz. cream cheese

2 cups sour cream

1 oz. powdered ranch dressing mix

½ tsp. garlic powder

½ tsp. onion powder

2½ cups broccoli florets

5 pieces of bacon, cooked and crumbled

2 cups cheddar cheese, shredded

½ cup Ritz crackers, crushed

S ET OUT CREAM cheese until it is room temperature. Preheat oven to 400ºF. In a large bowl, combine cream cheese and sour cream. Fold in ranch dressing mix, garlic powder, and onion powder. Add bacon pieces, broccoli, and cheddar cheese. Put in large baking dish and sprinkle Ritz crackers on top. Bake for 25 minutes until bubbling. Let cool 5 minutes before serving.

When it comes to gatherings, there's nothing better than a classic dip. Every time I make this cheesy broccoli bacon dip, someone claims it's their new favorite. This creamy dip can be served with baguette rounds or toasted bagel chips or on top of a salted Ritz cracker, but my favorite is with warm, soft bread. Set this cheesy broccoli bacon dip out at your next party and watch it disappear before your very own eyes.

Cucumber Delight

1 cucumber, sliced
4 Roma tomatoes, sliced
1 avocado, chopped
8 oz. cream cheese with garlic and herbs
2 tbsp. basil
2 tbsp. mint
2 tbsp. dill weed
salt and pepper, to taste
olive oil

SALT AVOCADO AND cucumber and set out for 30 minutes before serving to pull out more flavor, especially if not completely ripe. I usually put them on a wooden cutting board and serve them on it. Layer cucumber, cream cheese, tomato, and lastly a piece of avocado. Sprinkle with basil, mint, dill weed, salt, and pepper. Drizzle with olive oil.

Nothing brings family and friends together better than tasty food. This light and refreshing appetizer has become one of our family's favorite. With us gathering around, cucumber delights disappear as fast as we put them on the serving board. However, if making them in advance, place the serving dish in the refrigerator lightly covered with Saran Wrap until ready to serve.

On a healthy note, not only are cucumbers a delightful treat to the palate but they also are extremely good for you. A cucumber is low in calories and has a very high fiber content. In addition, cucumbers help reduce the total fat intake from the digestive tract, resulting in less fat being stored. During digestion, the soluble fibers in the cucumber bind with fatty acids, allowing the fats in food to be efficiently removed from our body.

Granny's Southwest Dip

2 lbs. ground beef
2 packages taco seasoning
2 (16 oz.) cans refried beans
16 oz. cheddar cheese, shredded
1 onion, diced
½ head lettuce, shredded
1 tomato, diced
1 green pepper, diced
1 (4 oz.) can sliced black olives
¼ cup fresh cilantro

PREHEAT OVEN TO 350°F. Sauté ground beef with taco seasoning. Spread in oblong casserole dish. Add beans, cheddar cheese, and onion. Bake at 350°F for 30 minutes. Top with lettuce, tomato, pepper, olives, and cilantro. Serve with chips of choice.

This is my all-time favorite hearty appetizer dish. It just won't be a Mitchell gathering without it. I have started serving it as a young wife and mother, and before long, I have been asked to bring Granny's Southwest dip appetizer to every gathering I have attended. I have never served it when the entire dish is not scraped clean.

Italian Sausage Balls

3 cups all-purpose flour
2 lbs. ground pork sausage
16 oz. sharp cheddar cheese, shredded
14.5 oz. can Ro-Tel

1 onion, chopped
1 egg
½ tsp. Italian seasoning
¼ tsp. fresh garlic, minced
¼ tsp. fresh cilantro
olive oil

PREHEAT OVEN TO 350°F. Combine ingredients in a large mixing bowl, pressing mixture together with hands. Shape into one-inch balls and place on lightly greased baking sheets. Bake at 350°F for 25 minutes or until lightly brown.

Store uncooked sausage balls in the freezer for a yummy quick treat when unexpected company arrives. Bake frozen balls at 400°F for 18 to 20 minutes or until lightly brown.

These are the best sausage balls ever—so easy to make and perfect for every occasion. We like to dip them in ranch or barbecue sauce. And just to change things up, I sometimes put them in the slow cooker and sauté in marinara sauce—yummy. So if you're planning a gathering or heading to one, these Italian sausage balls are a perfect crowd-pleaser.

Little Mommy's Spinach Balls

4 (10 oz.) packages frozen chopped spinach
4 cups herb stuffing mix
1 cup Parmesan cheese, shredded
2 onions, diced
8 beaten eggs
2 cups butter, melted
2 garlic cloves, minced
1 tbsp. fresh thyme
salt and pepper, to taste

D.L. MITCHELL

COOK SPINACH AND drain, squeezing out all liquid. Place in a glass mixing bowl with lid. Stir in the remaining ingredients. Refrigerate for at least 2 hours. Roll into one-inch balls and bake at 300°F for 10–15 minutes until golden brown.

Spinach balls are such a memory trigger for me. The smell and taste take me right back to my grandmother's house every time. I can remember my grandmother, my mother, and me rolling, baking, and tasting "just one more" during so many holiday gatherings.

This recipe is great for parties because it makes almost eight-dozen spinach balls. It's also one of those that can be prepared ahead of time. You can freeze unbaked spinach balls on a cookie sheet and put into freezer bags for later use. Thaw overnight before baking.

Sweet Potato Wedges

6 long sweet potatoes, cut into 1″ × 3″ wedges
3–4 tbsp. olive oil
½ tsp. salt
½ tsp. pepper
¼ tsp. paprika
¼ tsp. garlic powder

PREHEAT OVEN TO 425°F. Place sweet potato wedges in a single layer on a rimmed baking sheet. Drizzle with 3 tablespoons of olive oil and toss to coat. If needed, add the additional tablespoon of olive oil to coat the potatoes thoroughly. Sprinkle on seasoning. Bake on 425°F for 18–20 minutes until tender and brown. If desired, place the sweet potatoes under broiler for 2 minutes for more crispy wedges. Be sure to watch them closely so they don't burn. I love to serve them with my favorite aioli-mustard sauce.

Need an appetizer or side dish everyone will love? Family and friends, young and old, will love roasted-to-perfection fresh sweet potato wedges every time. I like to cut large wedges, but the sweet potatoes can be cut into any size or shape according to the celebration. Season more or less as you please. The sweet potato wedges can also be cooked on the grill. I use a grill pan with holes in the bottom and place the potatoes away from direct heat, turning repeatedly as they cook.

Wontons

1 package wonton wraps
16 oz. cooked ground sausage
½ cup shredded cheddar cheese
½ cup shredded Monterey Jack
½ cup chopped red pepper
4.25 oz. can chopped black olives
1 large beaten egg

PREHEAT OVEN TO 400°F and lightly oil baking sheet. Combine sausage, cheeses, olives, and pepper in a large bowl. Fill each wonton with 1½ teaspoon of mixture, rub the edges of wrappers with egg, and fold all sides over, creating an *X*. Pinch wraps to seal. Bake for 10–12 minutes until golden brown and crisp.

These wontons are unbelievably easy and simple—perfect for a large family gathering or block party. No one ever believes these crispy, creamy wontons are baked, not fried. They are not only tasty but also a delectable alternative to the usual appetizers brought to any party. I usually make a large batch and freeze half in an airtight container. Wontons are great for popping in the oven at a moment's notice.

Zucchini Fritters

Dill Dip

1 ripe avocado, mashed
½ tsp. onion powder
½ tsp. mayonnaise
½ cup fresh dill, finely chopped
salt and pepper, to taste

Fritter

1 large zucchini
2 eggs
1 tbsp. lemon zest
1 tsp. garlic, minced
¼ cup fresh basil
¼ cup fresh oregano
¼ tsp. onion powder
¼ cup flour
2 tbsp. olive oil

S TIR DILL DIP ingredients together and place in the refrigerator to chill.

Grate zucchini with the large holes of a box grater. Place in colander and toss with ½ teaspoon salt. Set aside for 10 minutes and then wring zucchini dry in paper towel. Place zucchini in a large bowl and gently mix in egg, lemon zest, garlic, basil, oregano, onion powder, salt, and pepper. Slowly add in flour so no lumps form.

Heat 2 tablespoons olive oil on large electric griddle until oil sizzles. Carefully drop 2 tablespoons of the zucchini mixture into pan, spacing fritters a few inches apart. Cook until golden brown, about 3 minutes on each side.

I don't know if it's the taste or the name, but everyone loves zucchini fritters. It's the perfect appetizer to get the taste buds going. I like to serve cooked fritters right off the griddle or on a heating plate so that they are warm when served. But beware, the smell is so tempting that some just seem to walk away before I have finished cooking the whole batch.

D.L. MITCHELL

Berry Good Sangria

1 orange, sliced
2 cinnamon sticks
¼ tsp. ground cloves
½ tsp. ground nutmeg
1 cup fresh cranberries
4 cups apple cider vinegar
4 cups water
1 bottle Chardonnay

COMBINE FRUIT AND spices in a two-quart slow cooker. Cover with vinegar and about two inches of water. Stir and set on low, uncovered. Floaters will settle as they simmer. Add water as needed to ensure ingredients do not burn. Remove from heat and add wine once mixture cools.

I had this for the very first time at an international party in Boston when I was just a young thirty-year-old. Everyone said, "You've got to try it. It's delicious." I did, it was, and I had enjoyed preparing it on special occasions ever since.

Cleansing Detox Drink

½ cucumber, sliced
1 tbsp. freshly grated ginger

16 oz. water
1 lemon, squeezed
Himalayan pink salt

B LEND CUCUMBER AND grated ginger with water until
smooth. Stir in lemon juice and a pinch of salt. For extra zest,
add a few shavings of lemon rind or chopped parsley, mint, or cilantro
leaves.

This drink is not only light and refreshing but also a favorite beverage
of many people for weight loss. It's a great drink in the morning or as a
nice afternoon pick-me-up.

Cold Coffee Perk

black coffee, freshly brewed
1½ oz. vanilla vodka
1½ oz. Baileys Irish Cream liquor

L ET COFFEE COOL and pour coffee into two ice trays. Freeze
overnight. Place coffee cubes in a glass mug and add vodka
and liquor for a good old-fashioned afternoon perk. Recipe makes two
beverages.

I have enjoyed Baileys Irish Cream liquor for the first time in a long
time while visiting family in Oregon not too long ago. I have mentally
made a note to self: *Must share this fantastic cold coffee perk recipe when
I get home.* The name of this beverage says it all. It's a delicious perk
anytime, anywhere.

　　D.L. MITCHELL

Ginger Ale Sherbet Punch

½ gallon lime sherbet
1 (64 oz.) can pineapple juice
2 liters ginger ale

ALLOW SHERBET TO slightly soften at room temperature and scoop into a glass punch bowl. Add pineapple juice and ginger ale. It's ready to serve. For the adult crowd, add 1–2 bottles of champagne to the punch.

In the past, I would have told you that, just like my mother, I would always serve this punch in my grandmother's cut-glass punch bowl. However, recently, I have purchased one of those three-tier fountains with lights and used it for a baby shower. It makes for a very fun and festive centerpiece. Change is good. Just be careful of splattering punch. Next time, I will definitely use a tablecloth under the fountain.

Honey Irish Whiskey

2 cups water
½ cup local raw honey
1 lemon, sliced
2 scoop Country Time lemonade mix
resh lavender
fresh mint
Irish whiskey
Honey bourbon whiskey

HEAT WATER IN a saucepan. Once the water is simmering, turn off the heat and add honey and sliced lemon. Allow mixture to cool before adding lemonade mix, lavender, and mint. Add equal proportions of the whiskey and bourbon, 1 cup each. Chill the beverage and enjoy. This recipe makes a small pitcher, which can be served in chilled glasses or mugs. Multiply the recipe, and it can be served as a punch.

Don't go high end on the whiskey and bourbon; it gives it too much of a charcoal taste. I like to use Jameson Irish whiskey and Jack Daniels honey bourbon. Make it your own signature sipping drink with your favorite steeped herb—basil, lavender, mint, or rosemary.

This has been served as a signature drink at the Haylee Marie Mitchell and Michael Lindenau wedding reception at Metropolitan Club on April 12, 2014, and everyone loves it.

Jungle Tea

1 gallon water
2 red mango tea bags
2 ginger lemon tea bags
2 red chai tea bags
½ cup raw sugar

BOIL WATER AND brew tea bags together. Sweeten to taste.

When I lived in Johnson City, Tennessee, I frequently visited a tearoom for lunch in the neighboring town of Jonesborough. This tea was always my drink of choice, and one day I asked the server what was in it. She left the table saying she would ask and came back to the table with written ingredients on a note for me. As with most of the people I met in this cozy east Tennessee town, she was just too sweet. I continued to make this tea weekly and consumed most of it myself.

Lavender Lemonade

¾ cup honey
7 cups warm water
½ drop lavender essential oil (or ¼ cup dried lavender)
4 lemons, peeled and juiced
lavender sprigs for garnish

DISSOLVE THE HONEY in warm water, and then add the lemon juice and lavender oil. Stir well and refrigerate until cool. If you want a more concentrated version, try reducing the water component and then add sparkling mineral water and ice just before serving.

Oh my goodness, are you ready to smack your lips? This lavender lemonade is my favorite lemonade. It tastes fabulous and makes for an unforgettable, refreshing summer drink.

Mint Julep

2 cups water
2 cups white sugar
½ cup fresh mint leaves, chopped

10 oz. Jim Beam bourbon whiskey
8 oz. club soda
1 lime, sliced

COMBINE WATER, SUGAR, and chopped mint leaves in a small saucepan. Bring to a boil over high heat until the sugar is completely dissolved. Pour into a quart mason jar and allow syrup to cool in the refrigerator for about an hour. Strain leaves by pouring syrup through a strainer. Add bourbon whiskey to the mason jar and shake well. Pour into frosted pewter goblets or Grandma's short old-fashioned glasses, top with a splash of club soda, and stir. Garnish with a sprig of fresh mint and sliced lime.

I've enjoyed my very first mint julep at the Swan Coach House in Atlanta, Georgia, with my mother and grandmother. This drink, served with the Swan's special, is truly one of the best ladies' luncheon meals I have ever put in my mouth. It will always be among my most favorite times spent with these two precious ladies, whom I miss every day. Make any day special with family and friends with this special drink.

Nana's Favorite Blended Juice Drink

1 tsp. ginger
1 tbsp. honey
1 lemon or lime
½ cup apple, chopped
½ cup carrots, chopped
½ cup beets, chopped
½ cup celery, chopped
½ cup cucumber, chopped
1 cup fresh kale

1 cup fresh spinach
½ tsp. cilantro

CUT FRUITS AND vegetables into smaller pieces. Place in blender with ginger, honey, and cilantro. Add ½ cup ice and blend. I don't like my blended drinks too thick, so add twice the amount of ice for more frozen drinks.

Blended or juiced fruit and vegetable drinks have become quite the phenomena because they provide the vitamins, minerals, and phytonutrients of multiple fresh produce servings all at once. However, we have to keep in mind that many fruits contain more sugar than we realize, so we must be careful with the selection going into our drink. While I enjoy the refreshing taste of a blended drink, I have never been one to replace a meal with it. I consider it more of a special treat or perk, and likewise, I like to make sure that the fruits and vegetables I choose are providing specific benefits to me that I might not be otherwise consuming.

That being said, of my top three ingredients, my first choice is ginger, an anti-inflammatory that helps reduce water retention as well as increases metabolic rate, directly aiding in the fat-burning process. Being a carminative, ginger also reduces gas formation and relieves heartburn and other stomach discomforts. My second choice is honey, an antibacterial and antifungal that helps prevent cancer and heart disease, reduces ulcers and other gastrointestinal disorders, and helps balance blood sugar levels. Those who know me well would have guessed that my third choice will be apple cider vinegar. But I don't put ACV in any refreshing drink that I'm going to sip on. ACV is included in my morning routine as a shot, quick and easy. So my third choice is lemon or lime, an antioxidant that aids in detoxing, enhances immunity, boosts iron absorption, helps prevents kidney stones, and even fights off cancer.

I have fun alternating the remaining choices and have found that, just as with cooking or baking, certain things just go better together.

Generally speaking, I limit the drink to only one sugary fruit. These are examples of blends I like most together:

- apple, carrots, spinach, beets, lime, ginger, and honey
- apple, celery, cucumber, lime, kale, and cilantro

Santa's Good-Night Kiss

Elijah Craig bourbon
Amaretto
Amaro No. 4

MIX EQUAL AMOUNTS in your favorite sipping glass.

Santa's Good-Night Kiss is the drink to prepare after an exhausting night of wrapping presents and stuffing stockings. This sharp concoction is ideal at full strength. So to preserve the flavor and effect of this delightful sipping drink, use reusable stainless steel ice cubes. Every sip will take you back to a relaxing night in front of a warm fire after a long night of preparation for Christmas morning.

Summer Ice Tea Mojito

Muddling
8 mint leaves
½ cup sugar
½ cup water

Mojito
½ cup ice
1 oz. simple syrup
2 oz. white rum
¾ oz. fresh lime juice
½ oz. chilled club soda
4 oz. sweetened ice tea

F OR THE SERIOUS connoisseur, muddle the mint leaves using the following recipe: Combine water, sugar, and chopped mint leaves in a small saucepan. Bring to a boil over high heat until the sugar is completely dissolved. Allow syrup to cool in the refrigerator for about an hour and strain leaves by pouring syrup through a strainer.

When time is of the essence, the easiest way to muddle mint leaves or any herb is with a mortar and pestle. Simply put herbs in mortar bowl, sprinkle with a little sugar, and mash.

Add 1 oz. of simple syrup from muddling, ice, rum, and lime juice into a glass cocktail shaker and shake well. Strain into an ice-filled collins glass. Stir in ice tea and club soda. Garnish with mint leaves.

Seriously, this is the most refreshing alcoholic drink I've ever put in my mouth. The very first time I have been served an ice tea mojito from a pitcher, I've had to keep reminding myself there is alcohol in it.

Turmeric Tea Latte

1 cup coconut milk
1 cup water
1 tbsp. butter
1 tbsp. local raw honey
1 tsp. vanilla

1 tsp. turmeric powder

1 tsp. cinnamon

HEAT COCONUT MILK and water on medium-low heat until warm, about 2 minutes. Stir softly. Add butter, raw honey, vanilla, and turmeric powder. Continue to stir while warming for another 2 minutes. Serve with a sprinkle of cinnamon on top.

Packed with vitamins and minerals, this recipe makes two cups of the most delicious and health-supportive tea you can drink. And if you want your tea a little sweeter, add a little more honey. There's a very good reason turmeric tea is commonly known throughout the world as liquid gold.

Berry Overnight Oats

2 cups rolled oats
2 cups plain kefir
½ tsp. cinnamon powder
½ cup fresh mixed berries
2 tbsp. granola
1 tbsp. raisins
raw coconut nectar

MIX OATS, CINNAMON, and kefir in a large bowl and soak overnight. Serve with your favorite topping choices such as fresh berries, granola, and raisins. For a special treat, drizzle with raw coconut nectar, chocolate, or fruit syrup.

Kefir is a fermented milk drink that is highly nutritious and is one of the most probiotic-rich foods available. It can be made from any source of milk, usually raw cow milk, but it can also be made with coconut water. It has been proved to improve leaky gut syndrome and lactose intolerance symptoms, allergies and skin conditions, immunity, and bone strength.

Kefir-soaked oats are an amazing alternative to oatmeal or cereals and are crazy good for you. Scoop mixture into smaller containers for a quick, easy, on-the-go breakfast or snack.

Biscotti

3 eggs
1 cup blanched slivered almonds
1 tsp. almond extract
1½ tsp. vanilla extract
2 cups all-purpose flour
¾ cup raw sugar
1 tsp. baking powder
¼ tsp. salt

PREHEAT OVEN TO 350ºF. Spread almonds on a baking sheet and toast until lightly brown, about 10 minutes. Allow almonds to cool. Reduce oven heat to 300ºF.

Beat eggs, vanilla extract, and almond extract lightly together in a bowl. Combine flour, sugar, baking powder, and salt in a separate bowl. Gradually add egg mixture into flour mixture with an electric mixer. Toss in toasted almonds and mix. Shape dough into a 3″ × 12″ log and place on a lightly greased baking sheet.

Bake for about 30 minutes until firm to touch. Cool on wire rack for 10 minutes. Place on cutting board and cut into half-inch-thick slices. Return biscotti slices to baking sheet, cut side up, and bake for 20 minutes until firm. Flip each biscotti over and continue baking for 20 more minutes until toasted. Cool biscotti completely before storing.

Biscotti adds a delicious crunch to every cup of coffee or tea and is good to the last bite. For special occasions, drizzle dark chocolate over biscotti slices during the last 10 minutes of baking, but be forewarned—they will disappear before your very eyes.

Black Skillet Breakfast Bowl for Two

4 eggs
4 slices of bacon
½ cup grits or cubed potatoes
½ cup mixed vegetables
2–3 tbsp. coconut oil
1 avocado, sliced
oregano, parsley, and paprika, to taste
salt and pepper, to taste

COOK BACON, COOL, and break into pieces. Add coconut oil and seasonings to skillet and cook potatoes. Set aside. Cook mixed vegetables, adding more coconut oil and seasonings as needed. My favorite mixed vegetables in a breakfast bowl are broccoli, cauliflower, onions, and mushrooms. Cook eggs over easy. Toss in potatoes and vegetables. Add eggs and then top with sliced avocado and bacon pieces. I like to serve in wide soup bowls.

This breakfast bowl isn't just great for breakfast; it can also be served morning, noon, or night. I still consider eggs to be one of nature's most complete foods. Filled with protein and free of carbs and sugar, eggs are an awesome go-to snack or meal any time of the day. In recent years, egg yolks have been given a bad rep for its cholesterol content, but recent research confirms that the choline (the nutrient in egg yolk) is actually a belly-fat fighter and promotes cell activity and liver function. Although some folks fear the calories that come from the yolk and opt to use only the egg whites, I still favor sticking to the whole egg to get the complete nutritional benefit.

Gina's Berry Crunch Pancakes

1 ripe banana (slightly brown)
1 egg
3 tbsp. whole wheat flour
⅛ cup pecans
⅛ cup walnuts
2 tsp. cinnamon
1 tbsp. honey
2 tsp. chia seeds
2 tsp. flaxseeds
1 tbsp. coconut oil
half a handful of dark chocolate chips
½ cup berries of choice
¼ cup favorite granola
pinch of salt

MASH BANANA WITH fork and mix in egg and flour. Chop nuts into medium-sized pieces and fold into mixture along with cinnamon, honey, chia seeds, flaxseeds, chocolate chips, berries, melted coconut oil, and salt. Add a little coconut oil to heated pan and ladle a pancake-sized portion of mix into the pan. Cook for 3–5 minutes until edges are slightly brown. Add granola to the uncooked side and flip. Cook for another 3–5 minutes.

Honestly, this recipe is incredibly flexible. If you see something in the cupboard or fridge that you think will be a tasty addition, toss it in. If you are passionate for pecans, by all means, add more. If you simply want to make your usual pancake mix and add the granola before you give it a flip, that will work as well. I basically combined my favorite banana pancake recipe with a bit of inspiration, resulting in this delicious breakfast. It's healthy and extremely filling. I have tried several times using bananas at various stages of ripening and found that the best-tasting and easiest bananas to prepare pancakes with are those about 60 percent brown, but the inside isn't completely mushy. Also, my favorite berries to add are blueberries and cherries. I hope you enjoy.—Gina

This version of these awesome pancakes is inspired by Gina and me after stopping at one of our favorite breakfast spots after our five-mile hike around town, affectionately called the Dunwoody walking tour.

Nana's Breakfast Bites

10 ounces fresh baby spinach, chopped
1 medium Vidalia onion, chopped
2 sweet red peppers, chopped
8–12 eggs
¼ cup fresh oregano, chopped
¼ cup fresh cilantro, chopped
salt and pepper, to taste
1 avocado, finely chopped
½ cup chopped mozzarella cheese
salsa of choice

PREHEAT OVEN TO 350°F. Sauté spinach, onion, and sweet peppers in coconut oil. Set aside to cool. In a medium-sized bowl, whisk eggs. Add sautéed veggies, oregano, cilantro, salt, and pepper.

Rub muffin tins with coconut oil or organic cooking spray. Pour mixture into muffin cups, filling only three-quarters of the way. Add avocado and cheese to each cup, mixing gently. Sprinkle with oregano, salt and pepper, and bake for 30 minutes.

OMG, these are called breakfast bites but are perfect anytime. They also make for a healthy snack or appetizer.

Nana's Breakfast Casserole

12 eggs
1 pound spicy sausage
2 cups raw milk
1 tsp. salt and pepper
1 tsp. ground mustard
1 tsp. ground cinnamon
½ tsp. minced garlic
½ tsp. oregano
½ tsp. basil
1 cup bread crumbs
8 oz. cheddar cheese, shredded
2 cups sweet kale, chopped
14.5 oz. can diced tomatoes with green peppers

COOK SAUSAGE OVER medium heat and stir until crumbly and evenly browned, about 10 minutes. Drain.

Beat eggs in a large bowl, stirring in milk, salt, pepper, mustard, and cinnamon. Fold in bread cubes, cheese, vegetables, and sausage into egg mixture. Pour into a lightly greased 7″ × 11″ baking dish. Cover and refrigerate overnight.

Preheat oven to 350°F. Remove casserole from refrigerator for 30 minutes. Bake for about 45 minutes until a knife inserted near the center comes out clean.

This breakfast casserole has always been such a treat on Christmas morning, already made and sitting in the refrigerator, ready to pop in the oven while gifts are being opened. Add fresh fruit and the smell of freshly brewed coffee, and we are all set to enjoy the gift of sharing Christmas morning with family and friends.

D.L. MITCHELL

Crunchy Homemade Granola

¼ cup dark brown sugar
¼ cup peanut butter
¼ cup maple syrup or honey
¼ cup walnut oil
½ tsp. salt
3 cups rolled oats
1 cup almond slivers
1 cup pumpkin seeds
1 cup cashews
¾ cup sweet coconut, shredded
1 cup raisins

PREHEAT OVEN TO 250°F. Line baking sheet with baker's liner.

Combine dark brown sugar, peanut butter, maple syrup, oil, and salt in a bowl. Add oats, almonds, pumpkin seeds, cashews, and coconut. Mix well, making sure all ingredients are coated evenly. Spread on baking sheet, layering evenly.

Bake for 1 hour, stirring every 10 to 15 minutes. Crunch granola is ready when golden brown. Pour into a bowl while mixture is still hot and mix in raisins. Cool and store in an airtight container.

Such an awesome snack—morning, noon, or night. There's no better way to enjoy fruit or yogurt than with crunchy, homemade granola.

Oatmeal Bites

3 cups rolled oats
4 tbsp. ground flaxseeds
½ cup dried cranberries
½ cup dried dates
¼ cup coconut, shredded
2 tsp. cinnamon
1 tsp. salt
½ cup almond butter
½ cup honey
¼ tsp. vanilla extract
2 egg whites
3 tbsp. orange juice
olive oil

P REHEAT OVEN TO 350°F. Brush 9″ × 13″ pan with olive oil and line with wax paper.

Combine oats, flaxseeds, cranberries, dates, coconut, cinnamon, and salt in a medium bowl. In another bowl, combine almond butter, honey, vanilla, egg whites, and orange juice. Add wet mixture to dry mixture and stir. Press mixture into pan with fingers and bake on middle rack until golden brown, about 30 minutes. Let cool completely before removing from pan and cutting into squares.

Oatmeal bites are a great breakfast or go-to snack. Simple and delicious, these oatmeal bites are more filling than any sort of dry grain cereal. It does not have a ton of fiber, but with its ratio of four grams of fiber to half cup of dry oats, it's actually the powerful type of fiber that helps regulate our cholesterol.

Spiced Banana Nut Bread

4 ripe bananas, mashed
½ cup butter, melted
2 cups flour
1 tsp. baking soda
2 eggs
1 cup sugar
1 tsp. cinnamon
½ tsp. salt
½ tsp. nutmeg
¼ tsp. ground cloves
3 tbsp. honey
½ tsp. vanilla
½ cup walnut pieces

PREHEAT OVEN TO 350°F. Grease and flour two 8″ × 3″ loaf pans or one Bundt cake pan. Mash bananas and melt butter. Mix together the flour and baking soda.

With a large fork, mix bananas, eggs, sugar, cinnamon, salt, nutmeg, and cloves together in a large bowl. Stir in butter, honey, and vanilla. Fold in the flour mixture until no lumps remain. Add nuts to mixture and pour into the loaf or Bundt pans.

Bake until a toothpick comes out clean, about 45 minutes. Cool for 10 minutes, remove from pan, and allow to cool completely on a wire rack.

For a sweeter treat, add ½ cup semisweet chocolate morsels to mixture. I like to serve on a glass-covered cake plate and sprinkle with powdered sugar and cinnamon. It looks as sweet as it tastes.

DESSERTS

Affogato

3 scoops of ice cream (coffee, chocolate, or caramel)
4 tbsp. freshly brewed espresso or strong coffee
dark chocolate, shaved
hazelnuts, chopped

PLACE ICE CREAM in a coffee cup and drown with a shot of espresso. Top with dark chocolate and hazelnuts.

The taste of this coffee-based Italian dessert makes me daydream of the cafés in Italy every time. If the occasion calls for it, drizzle amaretto on top and serve with a biscotti. Sit back, relax, and picture your favorite café or vineyard.

Carrot Cake

Lemon Cashew Frosting	Carrot Cake
2 cups cashews, soaked overnight	1 cup almonds
½ cup fresh lemon juice	1 cup cashews
¼ cup pure maple syrup	2 cups coconut, shredded
1 tbsp. vanilla	1 cup almond meal
¼ cup water	6–8 carrots, peeled and grated
¾ cup coconut oil	1 cup currants
½ cup powdered sugar	2 tsp. cinnamon
	2 tsp. nutmeg

¼ tsp. clove, ground

1 tsp. vanilla

1 tbsp. lemon zest

½ cup dates

¼ cup maple syrup

¼ cup coconut oil

IN A BLENDER, blend cashews, lemon juice, maple syrup, and vanilla, adding just enough water until mixture is nice and smooth. Slowly pour in coconut oil and refrigerate while preparing cake.

In a food processor, pulse the almonds, cashews, and 1 cup of shredded coconut to a crumble. Place in a large mixing bowl. Add almond meal, second cup of shredded coconut, grated carrots, currants, cinnamon, nutmeg, clove, vanilla, and lemon zest.

In a food processor, pulse the dates, maple syrup, and coconut oil. Add this to the nut crumble and mix together. Use organic baking spray or parchment paper to line a 9″ × 13″ baking dish or two smaller ones.

Starting with the carrot cake mix, smooth out one layer of cake mix and cashew cream in dish. Place in the freezer for 15 minutes and then add another layer of each. Put in the freezer, preferably overnight, to set. Place on your prettiest glass cake dish and sprinkle with powdered sugar, a few grated carrot pieces, and lemon zest.

Hands down, it's a winner every time. Who doesn't love carrot cake, one of the best comfort foods ever created? This carrot cake is moist and delicious, made with lots of fresh carrots, and topped with the most heavenly lemon frosting. This is yet another memory trigger of time spent together around the table during the holidays, with family and friends reminiscing the past and anticipating the future.

Chocolate-Chip Zucchini Bread

2 cups zucchini, grated
1 cup tapioca flour
½ cup oat flour
¾ cup almond meal
½ cup coconut sugar
1 cup dark chocolate chips
½ tsp. baking soda
½ tsp. baking powder
½ tsp. salt
1 tsp. vanilla extract
¼ cup coconut oil
3 eggs

PREHEAT OVEN TO 300°F. Butter or spray loaf pan with organic baking spray.

Grate zucchini and squeeze out excess water with clean paper towel. Blend flours, almond meal, sugar, and chocolate chips in a large bowl. Whisk in baking soda, baking powder, and salt until well blended. Add vanilla, coconut oil, and eggs to bowl and mix evenly. Pour mixture into loaf pan and bake for 35–45 minutes. Let stand for 10 minutes before serving.

Why is it when you add chocolate chips to any recipe, it suddenly becomes the best thing you've ever put in your mouth? Seriously, it's a taste bud pleaser. If, like me, it becomes one of those loaves you just have to share with family and friends, buy festive seasonal loaf pans and keep a few in the freezer.

Fruit Tart

1 package refrigerated crescent rolls
2 (8 oz.) packages cream cheese
½ cup sugar
assorted fresh fruits of choice

SOFTEN CREAM CHEESE and sugar and set aside. Preheat oven to 350°F. Flatten and bake unrolled dough on a nonstick cookie sheet for about 12 minutes. It's better to undercook than overcook the crescent roll dough. Let cool. Spread cream cheese mixture on cooled pastry and top with sliced fruit. Chill in refrigerator. Cut into squares and serve with Cool Whip or whipped cream, topped with small mint leaves. Fruit tart can also be prepared in cake, pie, or cupcake pans. For that extra special occasion, drizzle with your favorite fruity syrup or liqueur. Ooh la la!

I have always loved fruit tarts. But for many years, I have bought them ready made and ended up wasting much too much, along with all the other desserts that have not been eaten during a gathering. However, a few years ago, I have discovered they are way too easy to make with the Pillsbury crescent roll dough that is always sitting in the refrigerator anyway, and the leftovers can easily be stored in an airtight container for 3–5 days.

Irish Delight

2 cups miniature marshmallows
2 boxes pistachio Jell-O pudding
1 medium container Cool Whip

1 cup nuts, chopped

2 cans pineapple or mandarin oranges, crushed

Maraschino cherries

MIX JUICE FROM pineapple with pudding in a serving bowl. Fold in remaining ingredients. Cool in refrigerator for 4–6 hours. Top with cherries.

Irish delight is so light and airy. A palate cleanser and sweet treat in one, it can be served as a salad or dessert.

Being 100 percent Irish, my proud mama made this scrumptious treat every chance she got. Although she never made it to Ireland during her lifetime, my mom was the proudest Irish woman I'd ever known. She loved her heritage and enjoyed sharing it with others during her annual Irish fest on St. Patrick's Day, when she and her home were decked with everything Irish.

Mimi's Bourbon Balls

2 cups pecans, finely chopped

2 cups shortbread cookie crumbs

½ cup heavy cream

4 tbsp. agave nectar

2 tbsp. honey

8 oz. dark chocolate chips

½ cup bourbon (Evan Williams Single Barrel)

1 tbsp. vanilla

¼ cup sugar

½ cup powdered sugar

PLACE ONE CUP of chopped pecans and shortbread crumbs in a large bowl. Place dark chocolate chips in a medium bowl. In a small saucepan, heat together the cream, nectar, and honey. Bring to a boil and pour over the chocolate chips. Let stand for 1 minute and then stir to mix. Pour this mixture over the pecans and shortbread and add bourbon. Chill mixture for at least 1 hour.

Mix vanilla and sugar together in small bowl. Add second cup of pecans to mixture.

From the chilled crumb mixture, form teaspoon-sized, small balls and roll them through the vanilla-sugar-pecan mixture. Place on serving tray or plate and sprinkle with powdered sugar.

As a child, there was a special place for the plate of bourbon balls at the drink counter, which of course couldn't be reached by us children. We were never given more than a taste of a bourbon ball, but the adults sure enjoyed them. Now I knew why. Once Mimi (my sweet mom) took her famous bourbon balls to a party, she was asked to bring them every time. You see, Mimi took a little liberty with the recipe, and her bourbon balls were always made with a cup of bourbon rather than the suggested half cup.

Mimi's Lemon Squares

1 cup butter, softened
2¼ cups all-purpose flour
2 cups sugar
½ tsp. baking powder
4 eggs
2 lemons, juiced (6–8 tbsp.)
½ cup powdered sugar

PREHEAT OVEN TO 350°F. Blend together butter, 2 cups flour, and ½ cup sugar and press into the bottom of an ungreased 9″ × 13″ pan. Bake for 15 to 20 minutes or until firm and golden.

Blend remaining 1½ cups sugar and ¼ cup flour, eggs, and lemon juice. Pour over the baked crust and bake for an additional 20 minutes. The bars will firm up as they cool and can then be cut into 2-inch squares.

Mimi (my dear mom) loved to entertain her girlfriends. She would prepare tasty as well as pretty dishes and always served them on her cut-glass luncheon plates with matching teacups. Her lemon squares were always a favorite, served on a three-tier glass serving dish and garnished with powdered sugar and fresh mint leaves, always delicious and always a special treat. Growing up, many times, when the ladies had come for lunch and I got home from school, they were still gathered around the kitchen table. And when my beloved dad returned home from work, a few were still there.

Ooey Gooey Bars

1 stick butter, melted
1½ cups graham crackers
8 oz. semisweet or dark chocolate chips
8 oz. butterscotch chips
½ cup walnuts, chopped
½ cup pecans, chopped
1 can (14 oz.) condensed milk
1 cup coconut, shredded

PREHEAT OVEN TO 350°F. Butter 9″ ×13″ pan. Pour melted butter and graham crackers into a bowl and crush into small pieces. Spread graham cracker crumbs in bottom of pan. Layer chocolate and butterscotch chips and nuts over formed crumbs. Pour condensed milk on top and sprinkle with shredded coconut. Bake for 25 minutes. Cool before cutting.

D.L. MITCHELL

And if you're looking for extraspecial cookies to bring to a gathering, just scoop mixture into rounded tablespoons and place on a cookie sheet. Bake at 325°F for 12–15 minutes.

These have always been my all-time favorite dessert. Everyone always seems to save room for one ooey gooey bar, even if they're stuffed from the most delectable party or gathering ever. A favorite variation of this bar is the ooey gooey lemon bar. Just substitute the chocolate and butterscotch chips with 6 tbsp. lemon juice.

New Year Clusters

8 oz. semisweet or dark chocolate chips
8 oz. butterscotch chips
2 cups Planters mixed peanuts
1½ cups La Choy chow mein noodles

Melt chips in a large saucepan. Add nuts and chow mein noodles and mix together. Scoop tablespoons onto wax paper. Place in the refrigerator for several hours to set. Enjoy. Bet you can't eat just one.

The first time I saw my grandmother and mother put these four simple ingredients on the counter, I agreed they all made great snack foods, but I couldn't believe we were going to put chow mein noodles on anything but Chinese food. Once again, mother (and grandmother) always knows best, and this recipe has been one of our family's favorites for as long as I can remember.

Peanut Butter Buckeyes

¾ cup butter, melted
3½ cup powdered sugar

1½ cup creamy peanut butter
1 tsp. vanilla
12 oz. 60 percent cacao Ghirardelli melting wafers or baking chips

I N A LARGE mixing bowl, blend melted butter, powdered sugar, peanut butter, and vanilla until smooth. Scoop mixture and roll into heaping teaspoon-sized balls. Place on a wax-paper-lined baking sheet and refrigerate for about an hour.

Melt chocolate. Pick up chilled balls with toothpicks, dipping bottoms into melted chocolate (leaving peanut butter top exposed). Place back on wax paper and allow to set.

Toothpicks can be left on buckeyes for serving, or if desired, remove and pinch and pat until hole is smooth. Buckeyes melt in your mouth, much like a Reese's peanut butter cup.

I'd never forget the first time I had a peanut butter buckeye. Ironically, it was at an international family gathering of more than one hundred at our home in Boston, Massachusetts. As a young married couple, we were fortunate to live in the one and only historical and beautiful Beantown for a year, along with fifty other Sloan fellows and their families from around the world. It was actually another Southerner from Birmingham, Alabama, who brought the buckeyes to the family picnic. I, along with many other international transplants, fell in love with Boston, baked beans, and buckeyes that year.

And here, I had to include a little tidbit that I learned while living there. Although the locals of Greater Boston refer to the downtown core as the city, traders and sailors during the colonial days nicknamed it Beantown for their love of the favored regional dish of Boston baked beans, which was nothing more than beans baked in molasses for several hours. And I would be remiss if I didn't share that the love of baked beans continued on in our family. Our precious David and Liam (sons of Haylee and Mike) loved baked beans with their "eggies" in the morning.

Terri's Texas Chocolate Cake

Cake

2 cups flour
2 cups sugar
¼ tsp. salt
2 sticks butter, melted
¼ cup cocoa
1 cup boiling water
½ cup buttermilk
2 eggs
1 tsp. baking soda
1 tsp. vanilla

Icing

1 stick butter, melted
4 tbsp. cocoa
6 tbsp. milk
1 tsp. vanilla
1 lb. powdered sugar
½ cup chopped pecans

MIX TOGETHER FLOUR, sugar, and salt in a mixing bowl and set cake mixture aside. In a saucepan, melt butter and add cocoa and boiling water. Allow mixture to boil for 30 seconds and turn off heat. Pour over cake mixture and stir lightly until cool. Pour buttermilk, beaten eggs, baking soda, and vanilla into a measuring cup. Stir buttermilk mixture into cake mixture and pour into sheet cake pan. Bake at 350°F for 20 minutes.

While cake is baking, make the icing. Melt butter in a saucepan and add cocoa. Stir until mixed and then turn heat off. Stir in milk, vanilla, powdered sugar, and nuts. Pour over warm cake. Cut into squares, eat, and enjoy.

While still in college, I went to visit my good friend Terri, who had moved to Dallas, Texas. Terri was married and keeping a beautiful home for her and her husband. To my delight, she prepared a chocolate cake for dessert one night. I'd been making what I affectionately called Terri's Texas chocolate cake ever since. Although we lived in the same town for a very short period, Terri and her parents came into my life when I needed them most, and they would always be very dear to me.

Butternut Squash Casserole

1 tbsp. olive oil

2 lbs. butternut squash, peeled and cubed

½ cup water

6–8 amaretti cookies

2 lbs. lean ground beef

½ cup onion, chopped

½ tsp. oregano

½ stick butter

¼ cup all-purpose flour

3 cups whole milk

½ tsp. nutmeg

9 lasagna noodles

¾ cup fresh basil leaves

2 cups shredded mozzarella

½ cup Parmesan, grated

salt and pepper, to taste

HEAT OLIVE OIL in iron skillet over medium heat. Add squash, sprinkle with salt and pepper, and toss to coat. Add water, cover skillet, and simmer for 20 minutes until squash is tender, stirring occasionally. Cool and pour into food processor. Add amaretti cookies and blend until puree is smooth.

Cook and drain beef with onions, oregano, salt, and pepper. Cook and drain lasagna. Melt butter in a large skillet. Add flour and stir, gradually adding in milk. Bring to a boil over medium heat and simmer on low heat for about 5 minutes until sauce thickens. Add a pinch of nutmeg and allow to cool. Add puree and ground beef to skillet. Stir in a pinch of salt and pepper.

Spread a quarter of the prepared puree beef mixture in a 9″ ×13″ buttered glass baking dish and place 3 lasagna noodles on top. Repeat layering twice. Sprinkle mozzarella and Parmesan cheeses into mixture while layering. Save ¼ cup of both cheese and sauce for the last 10 minutes. Cover and cook casserole at 375°F for 40 minutes. Remove and sprinkle the remaining cheese and sauce over the casserole. Bake uncovered for 8–10 minutes longer. Let the casserole stand for 15 minutes before serving.

I love the sweet taste of butternut squash, but when my mother-in-law has first shared this idea of adding it to my lasagna recipe, I have been a bit hesitant. However, it truly is one of the most scrumptious tastes I have ever put in my mouth. Although I myself love to play with recipes, Granny has been the best at reproducing a recipe with her own flavor.

Chicken Divan

2½ cups fresh broccoli florets
2 cups pulled chicken
1 cup onions, chopped
1 cup mushrooms, chopped
1 (10.5 oz.) can cream of chicken soup
1 cup mayonnaise
½ cup cream
1 tbsp. lemon juice
1 tbsp. curry powder
1 cup cheddar cheese, shredded
½ cup bread crumbs or fried onions

PLACE FRESH BROCCOLI florets on the bottom of 9″ × 13″ glass baking dish and top with pulled chicken, onions, and mushrooms. Mix together soup, mayonnaise, cream, lemon juice, curry powder, and cheese. Pour over chicken. Bake uncovered at 350°F for 30 minutes. Top with bread crumbs or onions and bake uncovered for 10 more minutes.

Formal or casual, you can't go wrong with chicken divan. I've always enjoyed taking liberties with recipes, and chicken divan is no exception. I sometimes add bread crumbs or fried onions, but my favorite thing to do, especially during the wintertime, is add campanelle pasta. Just cook up 16 ounces of your favorite pasta and add to the baking dish before adding wet soup mixture. It makes so much that I have to use a second 9″ × 13″ baking dish—one for now, one for later. Serve with crème brûlée for dessert. It's a ten every time.

Chicken Marsala

¼ cup all-purpose flour
½ tsp. salt
¼ tsp. black pepper
½ tsp. oregano
4 skinless, boneless chicken breasts
4 tbsp. butter
4 tbsp. olive oil
1 cup mushrooms, sliced
½ cup Marsala wine
¼ cup cooking sherry

MIX TOGETHER FLOUR, salt, pepper, and oregano in a ziplock bag. Coat chicken breasts evenly with flour mixture, shaking off excess. Set aside.

In a large skillet, heat oil over medium heat. Brown chicken in the pan, about 2–3 minutes per side. Set on a clean plate. Melt butter in skillet and sauté the mushrooms about 5 minutes. Add Marsala wine and sherry and simmer for 2 more minutes. Place browned chicken breasts in skillet, turn once, and simmer until juices run clear, anywhere from 5 to 10 more minutes depending on thickness. For a light and healthy meal, serve with fresh asparagus and wild brown rice.

Chicken can be made in so many ways. One simple and casual way to cook chicken breasts is Marsala-style. There is nothing more enjoyable than standing over the stove with loved ones and a glass of wine while chatting and watching the chicken turn tender, moist, and tasty. Add a little background music, and the atmosphere is set for a delightful evening.

Chicken Potpie

3 cups chicken, cooked and pulled
1 lb. baby red potatoes, cubed
1 onion, peeled and diced
2 carrots, peeled and diced
2 celery stalks, diced
4 tbsp. butter
2 tbsp. olive oil
4 cloves garlic, minced
4 oz. mushrooms, diced
½ tsp. salt
½ tsp. black pepper

⅓ cup all-purpose or white whole wheat flour

⅓ cup water

3 cups chicken broth

2 cups milk

1 cup corn

1 cup peas

1 tsp. Italian seasoning

COOK BARELY COVERED potatoes in boiling water for 10 minutes and drain. Sauté onion, carrots, and celery in butter and olive oil for 5 minutes. Add in minced garlic, mushrooms, salt, and pepper and sauté for an additional 2–3 minutes.

Prepare roux. Combine equal parts of flour and water in a mixing cup and whisk until smooth. Or combine in a mason jar, cover, and shake until smooth.

In a large stockpot, bring to a simmer the sautéed vegetables, chicken broth, milk, and roux, stirring frequently. Stir in pulled chicken, potatoes, corn, peas, Italian seasoning, salt, and pepper. Reduce heat to low and continue simmering for 10 more minutes.

One of the most popular family recipes of all time has to be the chicken potpie. With a hearty mix of chicken and vegetables, it's not only superhealthy but also supereasy to make. It also makes for a great recipe for the slow cooker. Leave in the morning and come home to the delightful aroma of cooked chicken and vegetables.

Dan's Steak Marinade

½ cup Worcestershire sauce

½ cup soy sauce

¼ cup brown sugar

¼ olive oil

2 tsp. garlic cloves, minced

1 tsp. powdered ginger

2 tbsp. steak seasoning

½ tsp. salt

½ tsp. pepper

Combine all ingredients in a mason jar and shake well.

PLACE YOUR FAVORITE steaks in a 9″ × 11″ glass baking dish. Pour marinade until steaks are covered. Cover dish and marinate in the refrigerator for 24 hours. The remaining marinade can be kept in the refrigerator for up to a week. It's great on just about every dish—meat or poultry, vegetable or rice.

My grandfather James Dan Ryan was one of the coolest grandfathers ever. He was a handsome, intelligent, and quiet man who was admired and respected by everyone who knew him. I had so many wonderful memories of him and my adorable grandmother Delia Elizabeth Apker Ryan, affectionately nicknamed Bobbie. As a child, I spent many weeks every summer with them right up until I married. As a married couple with children, we continued to drive to Miami annually to visit Little Mommy and Dan until they passed.

Their home sat on one of the many little lakes in Miami Springs, Florida, and was always filled with family and friends. Some of my most favorite memories were cookouts in their backyard, where food and drink were plenty. Most cookouts included Dan's famous marinated London broil, cooked ever so tenderly that it truly melted in your mouth. As a young wife and mother, this was one of the first recipes I asked for.

Enchiladas

1½ lb. fresh, lean, ground grass-fed beef
1 package Old El Paso seasoning mix
salt and pepper, to taste
¼ tsp. garlic powder
1 onion, chopped
1 cup hot water
1 (6 oz.) can tomato paste
2 (14.5 oz.) cans diced tomatoes
8 oz. shredded cheddar cheese
8 flour tortillas

COOK GROUND BEEF and chopped onion with seasoning mix, salt, pepper, and garlic powder. Add hot water, ½ can tomato paste, and 1 can diced tomatoes. Allow to cool. Scoop 2–3 tablespoons of beef mixture and cheese into flour tortillas. Roll and place in a greased 9″ × 11″ glass baking dish side by side. Reserve 6–8 tablespoons of mixture for topping. Add remaining tomato paste and diced tomatoes to mixture and thin with a little warm water. Pour topping over enchiladas. Sprinkle remaining cheese on top and bake at 350°F for 30 minutes.

Although the enchiladas can be a meal in themselves, I like to serve with cilantro lime rice, fresh guacamole, and chips. Serve with a local IPA or margaritas, and call it dinner. It's always a favorite.

Guacamole
3 ripe avocados
1 lemon
olive oil
cilantro

Mash avocados and squeeze ½ lemon and 2 tablespoons olive oil into serving bowl. Sprinkle with lemon zest and cilantro. It's simple and tasty.

Kale Veggie Stir Fry

2 cups kale salad mix
2 cups broccoli coleslaw mix
1 onion, chopped
1 cup mushrooms, chopped
1 cup snap green beans, 1" cuts
2–3 tbsp. coconut oil
1 cup black beans or lentils, cooked and drained
1 cup salsa
¼ cup cilantro
salt and pepper, to taste

SAUTÉ VEGETABLES UNTIL tender in coconut oil, about 5 minutes. Add cooked beans, salsa, cilantro, salt, and pepper. Reduce heat to low until ready to serve.

Who doesn't love a simple, tasty, and healthy recipe all in one? Not only is this one of my favorite meals but it also is a great reason to pull out the electric wok. This veggie meal literally takes 15 minutes in total, so make sure your dinner guests are ready to eat. I have found that anything that sits in a steamy wok too long gets too soft too quickly for my liking.

Lemon Chicken Risotto

4 cups rotisserie chicken, cooked and pulled
1 onion, chopped
2 cloves garlic, minced
1 (4.5 oz.) jar sliced mushrooms
2 tbsp. butter
2 tbsp. olive oil
1 tsp. lemon pepper
1 tsp. lemon zest
1 package onion soup mix
1 cup long-grain risotto
½ cup white wine
1 (10½ oz.) can cream of chicken and mushroom soup
½ cup heavy cream
Parmesan cheese

IN A LARGE skillet, sauté onion, garlic, and mushrooms in butter and olive oil for 2 minutes. Stir in onion soup mix, lemon pepper, lemon zest, and pulled chicken and sauté for 2 more minutes.

Place risotto, wine, soup, and cream in a glass casserole dish. Gradually stir in the sautéed chicken mixture. Sprinkle with Parmesan cheese and bake at 350°F for 30 minutes.

Ultratender and moist, lemon chicken risotto is perfect for those nights when you don't really want to mess with dinner but need to wow the family anyway. Loaded with flavor, this incredibly easy chicken recipe makes everyone at the dinner table think you've been slaving in the kitchen all day. Add sautéed vegetables, and you've got a hearty option for a quick and light weeknight family dinner.

Minced Beef Lettuce Wraps

1½ lbs. ground beef
1 onion, chopped
¼ tsp. salt
¼ tsp. pepper
2 tbsp. apple cider vinegar
1 (25 oz.) jar of mushroom pasta sauce
½ cup hot water
½ cup bacon bits
1 avocado, sliced
½ cup poppy seed dressing

COOK GROUND BEEF and onion in salt and pepper. Drain. Add apple cider vinegar, mushroom pasta sauce, and hot water until slightly thinned. Serve in lettuce wraps, topped with cooked bacon bits and sliced avocado. Drizzle with poppy seed dressing.

Have you ever wondered what makes minced beef minced? Minced meat of any kind is simply meat that has been finely chopped with a knife or meat grinder. It is the perfect way to introduce meat to young children as it is easier to eat as well as digest. Minced beef is probably my grandsons' most favorite meal—that along with a little pasta.

As a young person, I've always thought *minced* refers to the fact that apple cider vinegar has been added to the meat. Go figure. If you haven't tried adding apple cider vinegar to your beef, try it. It adds such a unique flavor, and of course, it's good for you too. When trying to change things up, it's a great alternative to typical beef meals such as meat loaf, spaghetti, lasagna, and enchiladas.

When a more filling meal is desired, toss over angel-hair pasta. Minced meat can also be served as a side dish or soup.

Veggie Chicken Parmesan

4 skinless, boneless chicken breasts
salt and black pepper, to taste
2 tbsp. all-purpose flour
2 eggs
4 cups Italian bread crumbs, finely grated
½ cup grated Parmesan cheese
2 tbsp. olive oil
1 red pepper, sliced
1 yellow squash, sliced
1 zucchini, sliced
½ cup tomato sauce
1 cup shredded mozzarella
¼ cup fresh parsley, chopped
¼ cup fresh basil, chopped
¼ cup fresh rosemary, chopped
3 tbsp. olive oil

PREHEAT OVEN TO 350°F. On cutting board, sprinkle chicken with salt, pepper, and flour, evenly coating both sides. Beat eggs in a shallow bowl. Mix bread crumbs and Parmesan cheese in a separate bowl. Dip flour-coated chicken breast in beaten eggs and then in bread crumbs, pressing into both sides. Set aside for about 15 minutes.

Heat 2 tbsp. olive oil in a large skillet on medium heat. Cook chicken until golden, about 2 minutes on each side. Place chicken in a 9″ × 11″ baking dish. Surround chicken with sliced peppers, squash, and zucchini. Top with tomato sauce, mozzarella cheese, parsley, basil, and rosemary. Sprinkle with Parmesan cheese, salt, and pepper and drizzle with 1 tbsp. olive oil. Bake at 350°F for 25–30 minutes until cheese is brown.

Veggie chicken Parmesan is one of my favorite quick chicken recipes. Yes, it does add a few extra carbs to the diet, so make it the special treat that it is and serve only on special occasions. Since veggies are included, just serve with your favorite bottle of wine to make it that easy and satisfying meal that the whole family will love.

PASTAS

BESIDES THE BEST taste in the whole world, the best thing about pasta dishes is that the recipe can easily be doubled or tripled to feed a crowd, and most recipes taste great served cool or at room temperature the next day. Although some recipes call for specific pasta such as spaghetti or elbow pasta, my all-time favorite pasta is the campanelle. It is a bell-shaped pasta with petal-like edges that looks like a flower. It is also sometimes referred to as *gigli*. This twisted pasta holds more sauce and makes every pasta sauce and salad taste great.

It will be remiss of me if I don't mention here that while it is true that most pasta adds more carbs to a meal, one of the healthiest choices of pasta is Chickapea, which is made from only two ingredients: organic chickpeas and lentils. It is a superfood that's delicious and nutritious. With 27 grams of protein per 3½-ounce serving, Chickapea pasta has as much protein as an equal serving of steak. It also contains 35 percent of our daily recommended amount of iron intake and almost 50 percent of fiber. It's also full of antioxidants, probiotics, complex carbs, magnesium, B vitamins, and zinc. So if you just gotta have pasta but don't want the carbs, try Chickapea pasta.

Chicken Alfredo

3–4 cups rotisserie chicken, cooked and pulled
16 oz. penne pasta
½ cup butter
2 cups heavy whipping cream
4 oz. cream cheese

2 garlic cloves, minced

1 tsp. Italian seasoning

1 cup Parmesan cheese, freshly shaved

2 tbsp. fresh parsley

salt and pepper, to taste

COOK, COOL, AND pull rotisserie chicken. Cook and drain pasta and set aside.

In a medium black skillet, melt butter, heavy whipping cream, and cream cheese over medium heat. Add minced garlic, Italian seasoning, salt, and pepper. Continue to whisk until smooth, gradually adding in Parmesan cheese. Bring to a simmer and continue to cook for about 5 minutes or until it starts to thicken.

Place pasta and pulled chicken in glass casserole dish and gradually stir in Alfredo sauce. Top with a few sprinkles of fresh Parmesan shavings, parsley, salt, and pepper for the yummiest chicken Alfredo dish this side of the Atlantic Ocean.

This dish is excellent served with a light tossed salad, garlic bread drizzled in olive oil, and French haricots cooked in a little butter with onions and fresh garden herbs. It's always one of my family's favorites. If you know you will be pushed for time, stop by your local grocer on the way home and pick up a freshly grilled rotisserie chicken. By the time you're home, it will be cooled down enough to pull, and step 1 is already done.

Chicken Chili Lasagna

4 cups chicken, cooked and pulled

2 cups salsa verde

1 (10 oz.) can fire-roasted green chilies

¼ cup sour cream

1 tsp. salt

1 tsp. black pepper

1 tsp. cumin

1 tsp. chili powder

1 (15 oz.) crema

2 cups mozzarella cheese, grated

2 cups Mexican-blend cheese, grated

10 oz. lasagna noodles

PREHEAT OVEN TO 375ºF. Combine pulled chicken, 1 cup of salsa verde, green chilies, and sour cream in a large bowl and season with salt, pepper, cumin, and chili powder.

Place a third of the chicken mixture in the bottom of a 9″ × 11″ baking dish and cover with a layer of lasagna noodles. Top with another layer of chicken mixture and then cover with 5 ounces of crema and ¾ cup of mozzarella and Mexican cheeses. Repeat with another layer of chicken, 5 ounces of crema, and ¾ cup of cheese and top with lasagna noodles. Cover noodles with the remaining 1 cup of salsa verde, 5 ounces of crema, and remaining mozzarella evenly over the top. Cover dish with aluminum foil and bake for 25 minutes. Uncover and bake for another 10 minutes, until cheese is melted.

I must say that all lasagnas are a labor of love. And if you are in the second season of life as I am and blessed with time, go for it. Even the salsa verde is so much better homemade than what you get in a bottle. Homemade salsa verde is deliciously flavorful and makes a delicious topping to every Mexican or Southwestern recipe. Crema can also be store bought or made simply with a mixture of heavy cream and buttermilk. However, I must also admit here that I have never been a fan of sour cream, so if you like the taste of sour cream, you might want to add more. I have seen as much as ¾ cup added to the recipe.

Chicken Pesto Pasta

16 oz. campanelle pasta
1 (4 oz.) jar sun-dried tomatoes
2 tbsp. olive oil
1 bunch asparagus, ends trimmed and cut into 2" pieces
salt and pepper, to taste
4 chicken breasts, cooked and pulled
½ cup basil pesto
2½ cups baby arugula
Parmesan cheese, freshly shaved

BRING A LARGE pot of salted water to a boil, add pasta, and cook until al dente. Drain and set aside. In a large skillet, heat 2 tablespoons of olive oil or the oil from the jar of sun-dried tomatoes on medium heat. When the oil is shimmering, add the asparagus and sprinkle with salt and black pepper. Cook for 2 minutes. Then add in the sun-dried tomatoes and continue cooking for another 4–5 minutes until asparagus is done. Toss in basil pesto. Remove from heat, cool, and toss in a serving bowl with cooked pasta, pulled chicken, arugula, and Parmesan cheese.

This chicken pesto pasta will be one of the best meals you will ever make. I have never received as many "yummy" compliments in one evening as when I have served this at a dinner party along with homemade guacamole and Blue Chips; a relish dish of garlic stuffed olives, Kalamata olives, and sweet pickles; spinach salad; crescent rolls served with olive oil and shredded mozzarella; and gelato and warm butter cookies for dessert.

Creamy Spaghetti

12 oz. spaghetti
2 tbsp. extravirgin olive oil
3 cloves garlic, minced
¾ cup chicken broth
¾ cup heavy cream
1 cup shredded Italian cheese blend
2 tbsp. fresh parsley, chopped
salt and pepper, to taste

COOK SPAGHETTI FOR 8–10 minutes until al dente. Drain, saving 1 cup pasta water for skillet.

In a large skillet over medium heat, cook garlic, ½ cup pasta water, chicken broth, and heavy cream. Gradually add cooked spaghetti noodles, shredded cheese, and remaining ½ cup pasta water, tossing constantly until sauce reaches desired consistency. Garnish with parsley, salt, and pepper and serve immediately.

Creamy spaghetti is a great addition to any meal. It's simple, it's easy, and it tastes great. It is a true comfort food and a pasta that, I have discovered, is devoured by parties of all ages.

Nana's Mac and Cheese

3 cups elbow pasta
2 tbsp. extravirgin olive oil
½ onion, diced
1 tsp. garlic, minced
2 cups chicken broth

1 cup water
2 cups Fontina cheese, shredded
½ cup Parmesan cheese, shredded
1 cup peas, steamed and drained
6–8 slices bacon, cooked and broken into small pieces
2 tbsp. fresh parsley
2 tbsp. fresh basil
salt and pepper, to taste

COOK PASTA IN Dutch oven and strain. Pour olive oil in Dutch oven, and over medium heat, cook onions and minced garlic for 5 minutes, until lightly brown. Place pasta in serving bowl and toss with olive oil, onions, and garlic. Pour chicken broth and water into Dutch oven and stir in the Fontina and Parmesan cheeses, mixing until melted. Add peas, bacon, and melted cheese mixture to pasta and toss. Garnish with fresh parsley, basil, salt, and pepper.

The buttery, nutty flavor of Italian Fontina cheese is usually just slightly stronger than other cheeses but adds an awesome and unique flavor. If too pungent for your family's taste, provolone, Gouda cheese, or an American blend can be substituted, depending on personal preference. And for the ultimate crowd-pleaser, add a can of cream of bacon soup to the Dutch oven while melting the cheeses. Ooh la la, the creamiest and the best mac and cheese you ever put in your mouth!

Taco Pasta

16 oz. shell pasta
1½ lbs. lean ground beef
1 medium onion, chopped
1 packet of taco seasoning
¼ tsp. cumin
1 tbsp. brown sugar

½ tsp. salt
½ tsp. pepper
1 can (14½ oz.) black beans, drained and rinsed
1 (14½ oz.) can mild Ro-Tel
1 cup shredded cheddar
2 tbsp. cilantro, chopped
salt and pepper, to taste

COOK PASTA, DRAIN, and reserve ½ cup of hot water. Brown ground beef and onion in a large skillet. Add taco seasoning, cumin, brown sugar, salt, and pepper. Add ½ cup of water to skillet and simmer for a couple of minutes. Add black beans, Ro-Tel, cilantro, cheddar cheese, and then pasta to skillet. Simmer for 3–5 minutes until sauce is thick and creamy.

Taco pasta can be served right out of the skillet into soup bowls for a fun family dinner and movie night. I'm not sure if it's the shell noodles, the taste, or both, but just watch it disappear.

Tuscan Chicken in a Skillet

16 oz. campanelle pasta, cooked and drained
2 lbs. rotisserie chicken, cooked and shredded
8 slices bacon, cooked and broken into small pieces
1 tbsp. extravirgin olive oil
½ cup red onion, chopped
2 cloves garlic, minced
1 cup mushrooms, sliced
2 cup tomatoes, diced
2 cup baby spinach, cooked and drained
½ cup heavy cream
½ cup Parmesan cheese, shredded
½ cup water

2 tbsp. fresh basil
2 tbsp. fresh cilantro
salt and pepper, to taste

IN A LARGE cast-iron skillet, sauté onion, garlic, and mushrooms in olive oil. Add tomatoes, spinach, heavy cream, Parmesan cheese, and 1/2 cup water and let simmer. Add pasta and toss until fully coated. Add chicken and bacon pieces and toss. Garnish with basil, cilantro, salt, and pepper.

I didn't used to, but I have grown to love the big black cast-iron skillet. It simply makes everything taste better, and Tuscan chicken is certainly no exception to this rule. I love campanelle pasta, but for a slightly more formal dinner menu, Tuscan chicken is also great prepared with angel-hair pasta. You will rock the house with this recipe. Everyone loves it.

Vodka Pasta

4 chicken breasts, cooked and pulled
16 oz. penne pasta, cooked and drained
2 tbsp. butter
1 clove garlic, minced
2 shallots, minced
½ cup mushrooms, minced
½ cup vodka
1 (28 oz. can) tomatoes, crushed
⅔ cup heavy cream
½ cup water
½ cup Parmesan cheese, shredded
2 tbsp. fresh basil
salt and pepper, to taste

MIX CHICKEN AND pasta together in serving bowl. Melt butter in a large skillet over medium heat. Add garlic, shallots, and mushrooms and cook for about 3 minutes, until slightly softened. Remove from heat and stir in the vodka and tomatoes. Return the skillet to medium heat and simmer until alcohol cooks off, about 5 minutes. Stir in cream and water and cook until sauce thickens. Stir in Parmesan and basil. Toss vodka sauce into bowl with pasta and chicken. Garnish with salt, pepper, and sprinkles of Parmesan and basil, if desired.

Vodka pasta is a great change of taste and a new favorite for our family. This recipe can be simplified by adding store-bought organic vodka cream sauce in a jar and can be prepared ahead of time in a casserole dish. Remove from refrigerator while preheating oven to 350°F and cook for 45 minutes, sprinkling with fresh Parmesan and basil during the last 10 minutes.

Asian Chicken Salad

Salad	Dressing and Marinade
4 boneless chicken breasts, pulled	¼ cup soy sauce
24 oz. green and red cabbage, chopped	¼ cup red wine vinegar
16 oz. matchstick carrots	2 tbsp. ginger, minced
5 oz. kale, chopped	3 tbsp. olive oil
6 oz. almonds, sliced	1 tbsp. sesame oil
½ cup chopped cilantro	1 tbsp. sriracha
3 scallions, chopped	½ tsp. salt
1 tsp. white sesame seeds	2 scallions, chopped
1 tsp. black sesame seeds	
½ package ramen noodles, smashed	

IN A MASON jar, mix together soy sauce, ginger, olive oil, sesame oil, sriracha, and salt. Place chicken in a large resealable bag and add 3 tbsp. of the marinade mixture. Marinate chicken in the refrigerator overnight. Add red wine vinegar and scallions to marinade and chill in the refrigerator for dressing on salad.

Preheat oven to 375ºF. Bake chicken breasts for 30 minutes. Rest for 10 minutes before you pull them. In a large serving bowl, toss together pulled chicken, cabbage, carrots, almonds, cilantro, and scallions. Toss with enough dressing to coat salad. Garnish with sesame seeds and ramen noodles.

This Asian chicken salad with a dressing that doubles as a marinade has so much flavor that you won't be able to put your fork down.

Refreshing, crunchy, and delicious all at the same time, this giant salad is a meal in itself.

Chicken Caesar Pasta Salad

2 cups lemon pepper chicken, cooked and pulled
16 oz. bow tie pasta, cooked and drained
2 heads fresh romaine lettuce
½ cup scallions, chopped
¾ cup Parmesan, shredded
2 tbsp. fresh basil
1 cup grape tomatoes, sliced in half
½ cup Girard's light Caesar dressing

IN A LARGE serving bowl, toss chicken and pasta together. Add remaining ingredients and toss in Caesar dressing for the heartiest and most delicious salad you ever put in your mouth.

Chicken Caesar pasta salad is a salad everyone loves. It's a great meal to serve on a hot summer night when hot food just won't do. Light but hearty and filling, it's a salad your family will start asking for.

Cucumber, Tomato, Avocado Salad

1 cucumber
1 tomato
1 avocado
1 red onion

½ bell pepper
½ cup vinaigrette dressing
¼ tsp. dill
salt and pepper, to taste

CHOP VEGETABLES AND toss together in a serving dish. Drizzle with your favorite vinaigrette (Braggs is mine) or poppy seed dressing. Top with a dash of dill, salt, and pepper.

Full of Mediterranean flavors, this cucumber, tomato, avocado salad makes eating vegetables a piece of cake. It works with any meal and can be served on a romaine lettuce leaf, adding great flavor and appeal. For a complete meal in a salad bowl, add your favorite pulled grilled chicken.

Honey Mustard Chicken and Avocado Salad

Salad	Dressing and Marinade
4 chicken breasts, cooked and pulled	4 tbsp. yellow mustard
4 cups spring salad mix	2 tbsp. Dijon mustard
6 strips cooked bacon, broken into pieces	2 tbsp. olive oil
2 avocados, sliced	2 tbsp. local honey
1 cup cherry tomatoes, sliced	2 tbsp. apple cider vinegar
1 red onion, sliced	1 tbsp. garlic, minced
3 eggs, hard boiled and sliced	¼ tsp. salt and pepper

IN A MASON jar, mix together mustards, olive oil, honey, apple cider vinegar, garlic, salt, and pepper. Shake well and chill. Double the ingredients, and this dressing can double as your chicken marinade.

D.L. MITCHELL

In a large serving bowl, toss chicken, lettuce, bacon, avocados, tomatoes, and onion together. Toss with sliced hard-boiled eggs and a few extra bacon pieces. Drizzle with honey mustard dressing and let sit at room temperature for 10 minutes before serving.

This is the ultimate in tasty salads. The honey mustard dressing can be warmed and drizzled over salad plates at the table for those special occasions when you just gotta wow your crowd.

Lemon Orzo Salad

16 oz. orzo pasta, cooked and drained
1 pint cherry tomatoes, sliced
½ cucumber, diced
½ cup pine nuts, toasted
¼ cup olive oil
3 tbsp. fresh basil, chopped
2 tbsp. fresh parsley, chopped
2 scallions, chopped
2 tbsp. lemon zest
3 tbsp. fresh lemon juice
¼ tsp. salt and pepper

IN A GLASS serving dish, mix all ingredients and stir in lemon juice. Cover and chill for several hours. Stir before serving from bottom to top, adding a tad more lemon juice if needed.

Hands down, this is the lightest, most refreshing salad ever made. It's the perfect addition to any dish and the first one I select for a trio salad plate, along with chicken salad and cucumber, tomato, and avocado salad. The idea of a trio salad plate always triggers in me memories of my favorite tearoom luncheon spot that just we girls have frequented in every city we've lived in.

Mimi's Pasta Salad

1 (16 oz.) tricolor rotini pasta, cooked and drained
4 eggs, hard boiled and chopped
1 cup red onion, chopped
1 cup green pepper, chopped
4 stalks celery, chopped
1 can black olives, sliced
4 oz. hard salami
½ cup Parmesan cheese
¼ cup fresh parsley
4 tsp. sweet relish
1 tsp. dry mustard
1 tsp. celery seed
salt and pepper, to taste
¾ cup balsamic vinaigrette

IN A GLASS serving dish, mix all ingredients and stir in balsamic vinaigrette. Cover and chill for several hours. Stir before serving from bottom to top, adding a tad more vinaigrette if needed.

This is "that salad," the one everyone has asked Mimi to bring. I can still visualize her standing in the kitchen preparing this salad and watching her face fill with such delight when everyone has raved about it and asked for seconds.

Nicoise Salad with Salmon

2–3 lbs. salmon fillets
½ stick butter
2 tbsp. olive oil
¾ lb. small Yukon Gold potatoes
4 cups mixed lettuce greens
1 lb. French haricot string beans
½ red onion, sliced
½ lb. small cherry tomatoes, quartered
¾ cup pitted Nicoise olives, drained
2 tbsp. drained capers
12 fresh basil leaves
2 sprigs fresh thyme
4 cloves garlic, minced
½ cup Bragg organic vinaigrette
salt and pepper, to taste
4 large eggs

COOK AND DRAIN potatoes and string beans. Cook 4 hard-boiled eggs. Allow to cool. Slice or cube as desired.

Melt butter and olive oil in a black skillet on medium-high heat. Place salmon fillets, skin side up, in the skillet and cook for 4–5 minutes until golden brown. Remove the skin, turn fish over, and allow to cook a few more minutes until firm to the touch.

In a large bowl, combine lettuce greens, potatoes, string beans, onions, tomatoes, olives, capers, basil, thyme, and garlic. Drizzle vinaigrette over ingredients and season to taste with salt and pepper. Garnish with salmon and hard-boiled eggs.

Nicoise salad is my *favorite* and the one I always order whenever I go somewhere it is served. At home, you'll have an elegant dinner salad in about 30 minutes. I love to top it off with any fresh herbs I happen to have, such as parsley, dill, basil, cilantro, or thyme.

Red Potato Salad

8 red potatoes
8 slices bacon
2 onions, diced
½ cup apple cider vinegar
4 tbsp. water
4 tbsp. white sugar
salt and pepper, to taste
1 tbsp. fresh parsley, chopped
1 tbsp. dill weed
1 tbsp. basil

IN A DUTCH oven, cook, drain, and chop potatoes. Cook and crumble bacon in a black skillet.

Add chopped onion to bacon grease and cook over medium heat until brown. Add apple cider vinegar, water, sugar, salt, and pepper to skillet.

Transfer potatoes back to the Dutch oven and pour in remaining ingredients and toss. Scoop into serving dish and add crumbled bacon, saving some for the top. Garnish with parsley, dill weed, and basil.

I like to add red potato salad for variety and for filler, especially when serving a larger crowd. However, because of the carbs, many will opt out of potato salad when filling their plate. No worries, just make a tasty and delicious potato soup the next day with any leftovers.

Spaghetti Salad

Salad	Dressing
1 lb. thin spaghetti	¾ cup Bragg organic vinaigrette
1 pint cherry tomatoes, sliced in half	¼ cup Parmesan cheese, shredded
2 zucchini, diced	1 tbsp. sesame seeds
1 cucumber, diced	1 tsp. paprika
1 green bell pepper, diced	4½ oz. black olives, sliced
1 red bell pepper, diced	½ tsp. celery seed
1 red onion, diced	¼ tsp. garlic powder
2 tbsp. fresh parsley	
salt and pepper, to taste	

BREAK SPAGHETTI PASTA in half. Cook, drain, and rinse in cold water. Scoop pasta into a glass serving dish. Toss with cherry tomatoes, zucchini, cucumber, peppers, red onion, and drained olives.

To make the dressing, whisk together vinaigrette, Parmesan cheese, sesame seeds, paprika, celery seed, and garlic powder. Pour over salad and toss until coated. Cover and refrigerate for 3 hours. For best results, prepare the day before and refrigerate overnight. Toss from the bottom to top and garnish with fresh parsley, salt, and pepper before serving.

Spaghetti salad is a must for any occasion. With seasoned grilled chicken and bruschetta flatbread, this is one pasta salad that will impress. Although most of my salads are full of lettuce and good-for-you vegetables, sometimes you just have to bust out some carbs and go for something different.

Taco Salad

Salad
1½ lbs. ground beef
1 packet taco seasoning mix
4 cups lettuce mix, chopped
1 tomato, diced
1 can black olives, sliced
3 stalks of scallions, diced
½ red onion, diced
4 oz. sharp cheddar cheese, shredded
1 cup broken Blue Chips
2 tbsp. fresh basil
2 tbsp. fresh cilantro

Catalina Dressing
½ cup red wine vinegar
½ cup olive oil
¼ cup ketchup
3 tbsp. raw sugar
1 tbsp. paprika
1 tsp. celery seed
½ tsp. onion powder
¼ cup salsa

IN A LARGE skillet, brown ground beef over medium heat, breaking up into small pieces. Add taco seasoning and stir until coated.

In a large serving bowl, combine lettuce, tomato, black olives, scallions, onion, cheese, and ground beef.

To make the Catalina dressing, blend red wine vinegar, olive oil, ketchup, sugar, paprika, celery seed, onion powder, and salsa together in a mason jar and shake until smooth.

When ready to serve salad, toss dressing over salad and garnish with basil, cilantro, and Blue Chips.

I've always enjoyed Tex-Mex or Mexican-inspired dishes, but to be perfectly honest, I'm over tacos. A couple of really good bites, and then it's just a matter of scooping all the great ingredients back up off the plate. This taco salad not only is a delight to devour but it also has so much flavor that your taste buds won't know where to start.

White Chicken Salad

4 cups white chicken, cooked and chopped
2 eggs, hard boiled and chopped
1 cup celery, chopped
1 cup white grapes, sliced
¾ cup mayonnaise
¼ cup heavy cream
½ cup walnut pieces
½ tsp. paprika
2 tbsp. fresh parsley
salt and pepper, to taste

IN A LARGE serving bowl, toss chicken, eggs, celery, and grapes. Place mayonnaise and cream together in a measuring cup and stir together. Fold half into chicken mixture, cover, and chill for a few hours. When ready to serve, stir in the remaining mayonnaise and cream and garnish with nuts, paprika, parsley, salt, and pepper.

This good old-fashioned chicken salad recipe dates back to your grandmother and mine, and it's always a favorite. Our tradition is to serve it on a romaine lettuce leaf with cranberry relish and sliced kosher pickles. For a really elegant plate, lightly drizzle with balsamic vinaigrette.

Boston Baked Beans

6 cans organic baked beans
6 strips bacon, crumbled
½ cup maple syrup
4 apples, unpeeled, cored, and sliced
½ cup light brown sugar
½ stick butter
½ cup rum

MIX TOGETHER BAKED beans and bacon. Pour maple syrup on top, but don't mix in. Cover beans with apple slices, placing cut side down. Cream sugar and butter together and spread on top of apples. Bake at 350°F uncovered for 30 minutes. Pour rum on top just before serving.

Some may think that baked beans are just baked beans, but that's just not true. These Boston baked beans surpasses them all. I can hardly remember a Memorial Day, Fourth of July, or Labor Day cookout without these baked beans. Even if your crowd hasn't acquired the taste, they will when you add bacon, brown sugar, and rum to it. It's perfect with any meal and always a crowd-pleaser.

Cheesy Cauliflower

6 cups (1 head) cauliflower, cut into bite-size pieces
½ cup sour cream
½ cup mayonnaise
8 strips of bacon, cooked and crumbled
6 tbsp. fresh chives, chopped
2 cups sharp cheddar or Colby-Jack cheese
8 oz. jar mushrooms, sliced

PREHEAT OVEN TO 425°F. Cook cauliflower, just barely covered in water, for 8–10 minutes and drain. Combine sour cream, mayonnaise, half of crumbled bacon, half of chives, 1 cup of cheese, and mushroom slices in a large bowl and mix in cauliflower. Place in baking dish and cover with the remaining cup of cheese and bacon crumbles. Bake for 20 minutes until cheese is melted. Top with remaining 3 tbsp. chives and a few bacon crumbs.

I know I don't stand alone when I say that bacon makes everything better, but sometimes we just don't want the mess. Besides cooking bacon in a skillet, it can also be cooked in the oven at 400°F for 20 minutes.

I happen to be one of those people who loves vegetables. Raw, cooked—it doesn't matter. Bring them on. However, I realize that not everyone shares this enthusiasm for all things veggie. That said, try this dish on your family members who don't like vegetables. They will convert, I promise. It's like eating pizza without the crust.

Little Mommy's Baked Pineapple

5–6 slices bread, cubed
1 stick butter
2 eggs
½ cup sugar
2 tbsp. flour
2 cans crushed pineapple
1 stick butter

BROWN BREAD CUBES in melted butter and set aside. Beat eggs and mix with sugar, flour, and pineapple. Pour into round greased casserole dish. Top with browned bread crumbs and bake uncovered at 375°F for 30 minutes.

For those times when everything on the meal has to be extraspecial, grill 6–8 pineapple slices on low heat for an hour until they are caramelized and serve on top of baked pineapple with vanilla gelato and aged vinegar drizzle. Yowza!

We all have those favorite recipes that trigger memories of celebrations with loved ones, and this one is mine. As long as I can remember, Little Mommy (my precious grandmother), Mimi (my dear mother), and yours truly have served baked pineapple at every Thanksgiving, Christmas, and Easter family meal. It's the side dish that tastes like dessert and a favorite of all ages.

Nana's Stir-Fry

4 cups mixed vegetables (broccoli, cauliflower, carrots, onions, peppers)
¼ tsp. minced garlic
4 tbsp. coconut oil
¼ tsp. fresh basil
¼ tsp. fresh oregano
¼ tsp. fresh rosemary
salt and pepper, to taste
3 tbsp. Bragg organic vinaigrette dressing

PLACE COCONUT OIL, mixed vegetables, garlic, and seasonings in a large black skillet or wok. Drizzle with vinaigrette and cook for 6–8 minutes, tossing vegetables around every 2 minutes. Drizzle a little more vinaigrette on top, if desired.

This stir-fry can be added to any and all meals. In fact, it won't be a meal at Nana's house without her stir-fried vegetables. Again, all things veggie. Just change up the vegetables or the dressing for a different taste every time.

Slow-Cooked Scallop Potatoes

2 pounds russet potatoes, sliced thinly
1 sweet onion, sliced thin
2 cups boneless ham, cubed
2 cups sharp cheddar cheese, shredded
12 oz. evaporated milk

1 cup heavy cream
salt, pepper, and paprika, to taste

LAYER A THIRD of the potatoes, onions, ham, and cheese in the bottom of slow cooker. Sprinkle salt, pepper, and paprika on top. Layer two more times and pour milk and cream on top. Cook on low for 4 to 6 hours.

This is a side dish, and the ham is added for flavor, but it can almost be a meal in itself. Just add a sliced honey-baked ham and steamed broccoli. Game over. And while you're at it, do yourself a favor and leave the house while it's slow-cooking. Just wait until you walk back in the house and smell this meal cooking. Yum-yummy.

Spinach-Stuffed Onions

4 sweet onions
12 oz. package frozen spinach soufflé, thawed
1 cup Swiss cheese, shredded
1 clove garlic, minced
¼ tsp. salt
¼ tsp. ground nutmeg
1 tbsp. butter, melted

PEEL ONIONS. CUT a half inch from the top of each onion. Using a melon baller, remove center of each onion, leaving half-inch shells. Dice and set aside 1 tablespoon of removed onion. Place onion shells in a Dutch oven and cover with water. Bring to a boil. Reduce heat and cook uncovered for 10 minutes until tender. Drain.

In a small bowl, combine diced onion, spinach soufflé, ½ cup cheese, salt, and nutmeg. Brush the onion centers with melted butter and fill

D.L. MITCHELL

with spinach mixture. Place on a baking sheet. Bake uncovered at 375°F for 45 minutes until soufflé is set. Sprinkle with remaining ½ cup cheese and crumbled bacon. Bake 5 minutes longer until cheese is melted.

Without a doubt, everyone in our family will always have a fond memory of Granny's delectable spinach-stuffed onions. I don't remember the very first time she brought these to a family gathering, but I do remember thinking this is the best side dish I have ever put in my mouth.

And I had to admit that when I asked for the recipe, I thought, *Wow, this recipe is without a doubt a labor of love, and I hope Granny is willing to make this forever.* And thankfully, she was, and she did.

Sweet Potato Puff

5 cup sweet potatoes, cooked and mashed
½ tsp. salt
1 (9 oz.) can crushed pineapple, undrained
8 large marshmallows
¼ cup brown sugar
¼ cup pecan pieces

SPRINKLE SALT ON mashed sweet potatoes and blend in crushed pineapple. Spread half the sweet potato mixture into a 2-quart round lightly greased casserole dish. Top with marshmallows. Spread second half of mixture on top and cover with brown sugar and pecan pieces. Cover and bake at 350°F for 30 minutes.

This is one of those side dishes that everyone at the table loves. The marshmallows can be substituted with marshmallow cream, but if your child or grandchild is helping you prepare, pushing those marshmallows in the mixture is almost as fun as eating a few. It's so yummy that it's hard not to call it dessert.

Tater Tot Casserole

1 lb. ground beef
½ cup chopped onion
2 cups grilled vegetables
2 tbsp. coconut oil
8 oz. sharp cheddar cheese
1 can cream of mushroom soup
1 tbsp. Worcestershire sauce
3 cups tater tots, frozen

COOK BEEF AND onion in a skillet until brown. Pour off fat and set aside. Cook vegetables in a separate skillet in coconut oil. Stir soup and Worcestershire into beef mixture. Spoon beef mixture into a 2-quart baking dish. Add layers of cheese and vegetables. Then arrange the tater tops around the outside edges of the baking dish. Bake at 425°F for 25 minutes until potatoes are golden brown.

This is such a fun dish. Not only does it taste great but it also looks great. I like to use an oval 9″ × 13″ glass dish because then it looks like it's all about the tater tots, but actually, there are almost as many vegetables as potatoes in this dish. Put a few burgers or chicken breasts on the grill and call it a meal, perfect for those light dinners on hot summer nights.

D.L. MITCHELL

Chunky Creole Soup

1 onion, diced
4 cloves garlic, minced
2 quarts beef broth
½ tsp. chili pepper powder
½ tsp. cayenne pepper
½ tsp. coriander
½ tsp. cumin
½ tsp. oregano
½ tsp. sea salt
½ tsp. black pepper
3 + 1 cups kale, chopped
2 cups black beans, cooked and drained
1 cup tomatoes, diced
8 sausage links, cooked and sliced
1 cup black rice, cooked and drained
1 cup quinoa, cooked and drained
1 cup cheddar, shredded
1 cup Blue Chips, crumbled

IN A DUTCH oven or slow cooker, sauté garlic and onion in 2 tbsp. beef broth for 2–3 minutes. Add remaining broth, chili pepper powder, cayenne pepper, coriander, cumin, oregano, salt, and pepper. Stir in 3 cups of kale, black beans, tomatoes, sausage, rice, and quinoa. Simmer on low for 15–20 minutes. Sprinkle 1 cup of fresh kale on warm soup. Pour into individual soup bowls and garnish with shredded cheddar and crumbled Blue Chips.

If seasonings don't make all the difference in the world, then I don't know what does. This soup is bursting with flavor, and although you might want to add a few more of your favorite things, you won't want to leave a single ingredient out of this chunky creole soup.

Creamy Broccoli Cheese Soup

2 tbsp. olive oil
1 onion, diced
2 stalks of celery, diced
4 cups fresh broccoli florets, steamed and drained
2 cups chicken broth
1 cup coconut milk
salt and pepper, to taste
¼ cup feta cheese

IN A DUTCH oven, heat oil over medium heat. Sauté onion and celery for 3–5 minutes until tender. Add celery and broccoli florets. Sauté for 2 more minutes. Add chicken broth and coconut milk and bring to a boil. Add salt and pepper to taste. Reduce heat, cover, and simmer for about 20 minutes. When vegetables are tender, pour mixture into a blender and puree until smooth. Return soup to Dutch oven to keep warm. Serve soup garnished with feta cheese crumbles and fresh broccoli florets.

Creamy broccoli cheese soup is one of our favorite soups. It's deliciously thick and creamy, flavorful, and full of healthy broccoli. I love coconut milk, but if you prefer almond milk, go for it. This is one of those soup recipes that could taste just a little different every time, depending on the needs and desires of your crowd.

Detox Vegetable Soup

3 quarts organic chicken broth
2 onions, diced
2 tomatoes, diced
1 head cabbage, diced
2 cups spinach, diced
2 peppers, diced
1 cucumber, diced
1 tsp. Himalayan salt
1 tsp. black pepper
1 tsp. cayenne pepper
1 tsp. cumin
1 tsp. turmeric
1 tbsp. olive oil
2 tbsp. fresh basil
2 tbsp. fresh parsley

POUR CHICKEN BROTH in a Dutch oven or slow cooker and add the entire list of ingredients, making sure there is enough broth to cover everything. Continue to simmer until all veggies are tender, about 1 hour. Garnish with fresh parsley and avocado slices.

I have never believed in crash dieting or detox liquid diets that last for days, but I do believe in eating healthy regularly. That being said, we're all human, and we all put things in our mouth that we later regret. So if your desire is to truly detox your system in a healthy way, I hardily suggest a three- to five-day vegetable soup detox. On the fourth or fifth day, add 2 cups of cooked white chicken to the soup for added protein.

At the end of the week, you will feel cleansed and energetic and won't be craving everything in sight.

Energy Kale Soup

1 onion, chopped
1 cup mushrooms, chopped
4 cloves garlic, minced
2 quarts chicken broth
2 cups carrots, diced
1 cup celery, diced
1½ lbs. red potatoes, cooked and cubed
1 can Ro-Tel
2 cans white navy beans
3 cups kale, chopped
¼ tsp. fresh thyme
¼ tsp. fresh sage
¼ tsp. fresh cilantro
¼ tsp. fresh basil
salt and pepper, to taste

IN A LARGE Dutch oven pan, sauté onion, mushrooms, and garlic in 2 tbsp. chicken broth. Add remaining broth, carrots, celery, and potatoes. Bring to a boil, reduce heat, and simmer until tender for about 10 minutes. Add Ro-Tel, white navy beans, kale, and herbs and simmer for 5 more minutes.

This soup is superclean and healthy except for the potatoes. What can I say? I love red potatoes, yet I rarely eat them. Likewise, I prefer to add them to this soup. However, they can easily be substituted with your favorite cup of cooked lentils, rice, or pasta.

Ham and Potato Comfort Soup

4 slices of bacon
1 cup celery, diced
1 cup red onion, diced
3 lbs. red potatoes, cooked and sliced
4 cups chicken broth
½ tsp. salt
½ tsp. black pepper
2 tbsp. flour
2 cups milk
2 cups ham, cooked and cubed
4 oz. cheddar cheese, shredded
2 tsp. fresh chives, diced

COOK BACON IN a large skillet until crisp. Remove bacon from pan, cool, and crumble bacon. Add celery and onion to drippings in pan and sauté for 3 minutes until tender. Place sautéed celery, onions, and potato slices in a Dutch oven or slow cooker with chicken broth, salt, and pepper. Cover and cook on *low* for 20 minutes.

Prepare roux with milk and flour in a mason jar. Shake well and stir roux, ham, and ¾ cup cheese into soup. Continue to cook until mixture is thoroughly heated, about 10 more minutes. When serving soup, garnish with the remaining ¼ cup cheese, bacon crumbles, and chives.

This delicious ham and potato comfort soup is pure comfort food in a bowl. So easy to make, even finicky eaters will fall in love with this soup. I typically use raw milk and white cheddar cheese for this soup; however, any milk and cheese will do—your choice.

Hearty Tomato Basil Soup

2 cups water
2 tbsp. flour
2 tbsp. sugar
3 tbsp. apple cider vinegar
1 can Ro-Tel
1 (25 oz.) jar tomato basil pasta sauce
½ tsp. oregano
½ tsp. parsley
½ tsp. salt
½ tsp. pepper
1 tsp. basil
2 cups fresh arugula
2 lbs. ground beef, cooked and drained
16 oz. penne pasta, cooked and drained
½ cup Parmesan cheese, shaved

PREPARE ROUX OF water and flour in a mason jar. Shake well. Add to the entire list of ingredients in a Dutch oven or slow cooker and simmer on medium-low heat for 20–30 minutes.

Ready in less than 30 minutes, this hearty tomato basil soup is the perfect start to a meal or is a meal in itself. A couple of tablespoons of flour and a quick roux naturally thicken the soup with no need for heavy creams. When ready to serve, garnish with shaved Parmesan cheese and fresh basil.

Italian Tortellini Soup

2 tbsp. butter
1 onion, diced
3 stalks celery, diced
3 cloves garlic, minced
2 quarts chicken broth
1 can Ro-Tel
1 (15 oz.) can white beans, drained and rinsed
1 tsp. Bragg vinaigrette
2 fresh bay leaves
salt and pepper, to taste
4 cups of chicken breast, cooked and shredded
2 cups spinach
2 cups fresh cheese tortellini
2 tbsp. fresh parsley, chopped

IN A DUTCH oven, heat butter, onion, celery, and garlic over medium heat until tender. Add chicken broth, Ro-Tel, white beans, vinaigrette, salt, and pepper. Bring to a simmer. Add the chicken, spinach, and tortellini. Cook for 10 more minutes until tortellini is tender. Discard bay leaves and serve immediately. Garnish with chopped parsley.

Italian tortellini soup, filled with tasty and healthy ingredients, is one of my favorite soups to fix on a busy night. With ingredients purchased ahead of time, in just 15 minutes, the family can sit down to one of the creamiest and most delicious soups you will ever make.

CONCLUSION

N OT TOO LONG ago, a dear friend of mine invited me to her home for what she called a poetry night. What was this? For a class called New Theology and Culture, her response to an assignment was to plan a cultural event. Along with an evening of good food and good conversation, everyone was to bring their favorite poem to share. What an awesome opportunity to share something that truly made a difference in our life!

The poem that I immediately thought of and shared was given to me in 1983 at a baby shower for my firstborn in a little box set called "A Gift of Love." Oh, what a sweet, precious time in my life. I treasured this little set of books, worn and tattered as they were, and was grateful to have received the invitation to revisit this simple yet profound poem of Joan Walsh Anglund.

Thank you, dear friends of yesterday, today, and tomorrow, for giving me the gift that matters most. I am eternally grateful for your love and friendship.

Do You Love Someone?

Joan Walsh Anglund

The universe is wide and wonderful and filled with many stars.
The world is rich and varied and filled with many people.
And among its hundreds of towns, and thousands of homes, and millions of people, each of us is only "one" . . .
One small person in a world of millions of other people, in a universe of billions of other worlds.

Knowing this, sometimes we feel very small. Sometimes we feel lonely and lost, as though nothing we do can ever truly matter.

Each of us wants to be needed, each of us wants to be remembered.

Each of us wants to be important in his own special way. There are many different ways to be important in this world.

Some people become doctors and heal the sick.

Some become farmers and feed the hungry.

And some become teachers and share wisdom and knowledge.

But you can be a shepherd, or a shoemaker, or a baker, or a barber, or a captain, or a carpenter, or a king!

And whatever you are, there is still one thing that matters most.

Do you love someone . . . and does someone love you?

For the heart is its own world, and in that world you are important!

And that's what really matters, isn't it?

CREDITS

All Scripture texts are taken from The New American Bible, Revised Edition (NABRE). The Old Testament, 1970, New Testament, 1986, Psalms 1991.

My sources for inspirational quotes are many and varied. Collecting my favorite quotes has been a life-long pastime, and I have gathered them from many sources. Famous and notable quotes are identified in text and in credit list by author. Anonymous if author is unknown. All material in this book, other than that which is believed to be in the public domain, are copyrighted and/or credited to the appropriate entity. Please respect all copyrights.

All artwork within book provided by Barbara Genner, an artist trained in the Zentangle Method developed by Maria Thomas and Rick Roberts, Whitinsville, Massachusetts.

Cover Design is an original photo by Deanna Mitchell. Radnor Lake State Park, Nashville, Tennessee.

Foreword written by Jimmy Mitchell, chief curator of Love Good, a subscription company that empowers artists, patrons, and young people to raise their standard for media and build a better culture, and beloved son of Deanna Mitchell.

Foreword to Inspired Living Section written by Phillip Sidwell, Psychologist, Atlanta, Georgia.

Foreword to Natural Remedies Section written by Haylee Lindenau, devoted wife and mother, natural advocate, and loving daughter of Deanna Mitchell.

Foreword to Healthy Recipes Section written by Hallie Klecker, a personal chef, culinary coach, recipe developer, and podcast host specializing in health-supportive, allergy-friendly recipes.

Book Summary written by Kimo Kimura, DC, Perfect Health Wellness Center & Pilates Studio, Atlanta Georgia.

xvi Beattie, Melody. (born c. 1948) American author of self-help books.

xvii Kant, Immanuel (1724-1804), Prussian writer and philosopher. Something to Do, Someone to Love, and Something to Hope For. All rights reserved.

Pg 1 Seneca, Lucius Annaeus (c. 4 BC – AD 65), known simply as Seneca, was a Roman Stoic philosopher, statesman, dramatist, and satirist of the Silver Age of Latin literature. "When Shall We Live If Not Now?"

Pg 1 Seligman, Martin E.P. (2002). Authentic Happiness: Using the New Positive Psychology to Realize Your Potential for Lasting Fulfillment. New York, NY: Free Press.

Pg 5 Lincoln, Abraham. (180-1865) American statesman and lawyer who served as the 16th president of the United States.

Pg 7 Fully Alive Outreach. (2013) Founded by Deanna Mitchell, is an outreach offering collaborative resources, products, and services in Health and Wellness, Fine Arts, and Travel.

Pg 9 United States Catholic Catechism for Adults, United States Conference of Catholic Bishops, Washington, D.C., 2006. All rights reserved.

Pg 12 Mitchell, Deanna. Relationship Prayer.

Pg 13 In God We Trust, the official motto of the Unite States of America, 1868.

Pg 14 Just Do It, advertising slogan and trademark, Nike Shoe Company, 1988.

Pg 15 Shaw, George Bernard (1856-1950), Irish playwright, critic, polemicist and political activist. "The Single Biggest Problem In Communication Is The Illusion That It Has Taken Place"

Pg 17 Ruiz, Don Miguel, The Four Agreements, A Toltec Wisdom Book, 1997.

Pg 23 Post, Emily (1872-1960), American author famous for writing about etiquette. "Manners are a sensitive awareness of the feelings of others. If you have that awareness, you have good manners, no matter what fork you use."

Pg 26 Erickson, Milton (1901-1980), American psychiatrist and psychologist. "The Effectiveness Of Communication Is Not Defined By The Communication, But By The Response."

Pg 29 Carnegie, Dale (1888-1955), American writer and lecturer. "When dealing with people, remember you are not dealing with creatures of logic, but with creatures of emotion."

Pg 31 Hill, Napoleon (1883-1970), American self-help author. "Fears Are Nothing More Than A State Of Mind."

Pg 34 Grogan, John, American journalist and best-selling author of Marley & Me (2005).

Pg 34"All Dogs Go To Heaven," United Artists, 1989.

Pg 37 Pope John Paul II, (1920-2005), head of the Catholic Church and sovereign of the Vatican City State from 1978 to 2005.

Pg 40 Ruiz, , Don Miguel, The Four Agreements, A Toltec Wisdom Book, 1997.

Pg 41 "God Help the Outcasts," The Hunchback of Notre Dame, Walt Disney Productions, 1996.

Pg 41 Mitchell, Jimmy. American Speaker and Musician "The Battle," 2014.

Pg 43 Otiende, Ngina, certified marriage coach, author and blogger, Intentional Today.

Pg 43 Dunbar, Robin. British anthropologist and evolutionary psychologist, Dunbar's Number Theory on the number of people with whom one can maintain stable social relationships.

Pg 45 St. Teresa of Avila (1515-1582), Roman Catholic saint, Carmelite nun, author, and theologian of contemplative life through mental prayer.

Pg 46 Smith, Michael W. American Musician, "Friends," 1987.

Pg 51 Wilde, Oscar (1854-1900), Irish poet and playwright. "Be Yourself. Everyone Else Is Taken."

Pg 54 Dyer, Wayne Walter (1940-2015), an American self-help author and a motivational speaker.

Pg. 58 Ford, Henry (1863-1947), American captain of industry and a business magnate, founder of the Ford Motor Company

Pg 59 Auster, Paul (c. 1947) an American writer and film director.

Pg 60 Schueller, Stephen (1929-) Clinical Psychologist from the University of Pennsylvania, research focused on well-being, happiness, positive psychology interventions, and individualized intervention sequences.

Pg 62 Twain, Mark (1835-1910), American writer, humorist, entrepreneur, publisher, and lecturer.

Pg 65 Pilates, Joseph (1883-1967), German physical trainer, notable for having invented and promoted the Pilates method of physical fitness.

Pg 65 Kimura, Kimo, Doctorate of Chiropractic from Life University in Marietta, Georgia. Founder of Perfect Health Wellness Center & Pilates Studio.

Pg 67 Ueshiba, Morehei (1883-1969), martial artist and founder of the Japanese martial art of aikido

Pg 68 St. Irenaeus of Lyons (130 -202 AD), Greek cleric noted for the development of Christian theology by combating heresy and defining orthodoxy, one of the first Fathers and he was the first great theologian of the Catholic Church.

Pg 69 Saint Teresa of Calcutta (1910-1997), Albanian-Indian Roman Catholic nun and missionary, also known as Mother Teresa.

Pg 71 Franklin, Benjamin (1706-1790), American polymath and one of the Founding Fathers of the United States.

Pg. 78 Hippocrates (c. 460 – 375 BC), Greek physician of the Age of Pericles.

Pg 123 Edison, Thomas (1847-1931), American inventor and businessman.

Pg 125 Doerr, Anthony (born c. 1973), American author of novels and short stories.

Pg 213 Anglund, Joan Walsh (born c. 1926), American poet and children's book author. Do You Love Someone? (1971) A Voyager/HBJ Book, Harcourt Brace Jovanovich, New York and London.